Family Involvement in the Treatment of Schizophrenia

Edited by
MARION ZUCKER GOLDSTEIN, M.D.

Assistant Professor, Western Psychiatric Institute and Clinic, Pittsburgh, Pennsylvania

AMERICAN PSYCHIATRIC PRESS, INC.
Washington, D.C.

Note: The authors have worked to ensure that all information in this book concerning drug dosages, schedules, and routes of administration is accurate at the time of publication and consistent with standards set by the U.S. Food and Drug Administration and the general medical community. As medical research and practice advance, however, therapeutic standards may change. For this reason and because human and mechanical errors sometimes occur, we recommend that readers follow the advice of a physician directly involved in their care or the care of a member of their family.

Manufactured in the U.S.A.

The paper used in this publication meets the minimum requirements of American National Standard for Information Sciences—Permanence of Paper for Printed Library Materials, ANSI Z39.48-1984. ∞™

Library of Congress Cataloging in Publication Data

Main entry under title:

Family involvement in the treatment of schizophrenia.

(Clinical insights)
1. Schizophrenia—Treatment. 2. Schizophrenics—Family relationship. 3. Family psychotherapy.
I. Goldstein, Marion Zucker, 1932– . II. Series.
[DNLM: 1. Family. 2. Schizophrenia—Therapy.
WM 203 F1979]
RC514.F328 1986 616.89'82 86-1091
ISBN 0-88048-097-1 (pbk. : alk. paper)

5.95

Family Involvement in the Treatment of Schizophrenia

CLINICAL INSIGHTS

Contents

Contributors

Marsha B. Andrews, M.S.W.
Mental Health Clinician, Adolescent Day Treatment Center, Henrico Area Mental Health/Mental Retardation Center, Richmond, Virginia

David E. Biegel, Ph.D.
Associate Professor of Social Work, University of Pittsburgh School of Social Work, Pittsburgh, Pennsylvania

Leah J. Dickstein, M.D.
Associate Professor of Psychiatry, University of Louisville School of Medicine, Louisville, Kentucky

Ruth Drescher, M.S.W.
Program Coordinator, United Mental Health, Inc., Pittsburgh, Pennsylvania

Horatio Fabrega, Jr., M.D.
Professor of Psychiatry and Anthropology, Western Psychiatric Institute and Clinic, University of Pittsburgh School of Medicine, Pittsburgh, Pennsylvania

Marion Zucker Goldstein, M.D.
Assistant Professor of Psychiatry, Western Psychiatric Institute and Clinic, University of Pittsburgh School of Medicine, Pittsburgh, Pennsylvania

Janae House, M.S.W.
Coordinator of Outpatient Speciality Programs, Department of Psychiatry, Medical College of Virginia, Virginia Commonwealth University, Richmond, Virginia

Nadine Robles, Ph.D.
Anthropologist, Western Psychiatric Institute and Clinic, University of Pittsburgh School of Medicine, Pittsburgh, Pennsylvania

S. Charles Schulz, M.D.
Associate Professor of Psychiatry, Western Psychiatric Institute and Clinic, University of Pittsburgh School of Medicine, Pittsburgh, Pennsylvania

Mary V. Seeman, M.D.
Professor of Psychiatry, University of Toronto School of Medicine, Toronto, Ontario, Canada

Judith J. Stephenson, S.M.
Instructor of Psychiatry, University of Louisville School of Medicine, Louisville, Kentucky

Hidenori Yamatani, Ph.D.
Associate Professor of Social Work, University of Pittsburgh School of Social Work, Pittsburgh, Pennsylvania

Introduction

The study of the interactions between a schizophrenic individual and his or her family, and how these communication patterns change over time, has achieved ever greater significance for mental health professionals who attempt to care for these individuals. Likewise, the interactions among family members, between the family and the mental health system, and within groups of families who have united for mutual support have been identified as worthy of attention. The common goal of caretakers of schizophrenic individuals is to prevent or delay the occurrence of a relapse while enhancing the patient's optimal functioning in settings suitable to his or her individual needs. The achievement of this goal has now been shown by researchers working in a number of settings to be related to a combination of psychotherapy, chemotherapy, and social-skills training for patients; psychoeducation of families; and availability of community support programs for both patients and families.

This monograph illustrates the evolution of concepts as they have prevailed in the mental health field and documents the contributions that the insights of families of the mentally ill have made to clinical practice. It was primarily the courage observed in parents of schizophrenic children, especially mothers, that motivated me to bring together the contributors to this monograph. The 12 authors whose research and ideas are presented here have the unique credential of having listened to families' accounts of pain and of having stood by them, each in his or her own way, in the face of adversity. The contributors offer a variety of expertise in the areas of clinical practice, support systems, community organization, education, and research that others who work with the mentally ill and their families should find useful. We all have a great deal to learn from each other and to share with colleagues, schizophrenic patients, and the families of schizophrenic patients.

Bridges to unite researchers and clinicians, families and patients, and educators and students need to be firmly constructed. Some building blocks and blueprints are presented in this monograph. The question remains whether and how current developments in this field are conveyed to medical students so the wheel does not have to be reinvented with each generation. This question was studied by means of a survey of medical students and the study included in this monograph. As medical students enter the field of family practice in large numbers, it becomes even more critical to determine what their attitudes are toward not only psychiatry and the psychiatric patient but also the families of the mentally ill.

I trust that this monograph will contribute to ending the era in which psychiatrists have advocated for their schizophrenic patients a level of independence from families that only a few patients are able to attain because of vulnerability to the stresses of daily living. In addition, I hope it signals a growing commitment by psychiatrists to be available to patients' families to help them provide the support their mentally ill family member requires in order to diminish the need for institutionalization.

Marion Zucker Goldstein, M.D.

1

Families of Schizophrenic Patients: A Historical Perspective

Marion Zucker Goldstein, M.D.

1

Families of Schizophrenic Patients: A Historical Perspective

Past Theoretical Frameworks

Until recently, prolific and compelling writers and theoreticians had an enormous impact on the practice of psychiatry and approaches toward patients and their families. It takes about 20 years between the introduction of a major new idea and its entrance into general practice (1). Investment in established theories is so strong that the opposition to new points of view is almost directly proportional to the time it took to establish the old theories (2).

It has only been recently and only amongst groups not invested in established theories that definable results have become acknowledged as the only justification of a therapy and the ultimate confirmation of a theory.

Until two decades ago, theories could be established by observations of a few cases or a few families in depth and at length, and no one was much concerned about the ever greater significance of the sample size and ability to replicate findings.

I offer this review of theories not to find fault or be complete but to give credit to the gradual evolution in our thinking and the roots from which the current contributions highlighted in this chapter have grown.

It was Murray Bowen (3) who pointed out that more progress can be made in "understanding why we think about schizophrenia as we do than to understand why schizophrenic patients think the way they do" (p. 348). He also pointed out that it was better to pool information than to quarrel over partial concepts. One of his hypotheses was that it takes three generations of pathology for schizophrenia to develop as a failed attempt to adapt to the demands of growing up and as an expression of immaturity passed on by two previous generations (4). Out of this hypothesis then came the many interesting observations of three generations of families with a schizophrenic member.

It is important to note that it has taken 30 years for us to develop ways of helping families of schizophrenic patients that have an effect on the schizophrenic process beyond the effects achieved by drug therapy (5). Only recently have programs begun that are based on empirical research supporting the view that the family can be a resource and support for a schizophrenic person provided the family also has supports available to them. It seems that the difficulties that psychiatry has had, and still has, in dealing with its schizophrenic patients not only has been projected on the families but also became the beginning of an interest in family therapy.

Much can be learned by reviewing theories which have been misapplied at erroneous times and places in the lives of schizophrenic patients and their families. The much maligned schizophrenogenic mother of Frieda Fromm-Reichmann's era and separation–individuation theory of Margaret Mahler's era contributed unwittingly to the development of the parent-blaming approach in subsequent years. When Lidz and Lidz began their studies, they considered that the patient's dependency and symbiotic needs followed upon mother's inability to establish boundaries between herself and her child (6). They also hypothesized that the father may be the prime source for schizophrenia, particularly with daughters or with sons when father has strong homosexual tendencies (7). By 1967, the same authors described the schizophrenic patient as seeing the world according to parent's feelings, needs and defenses (8). The theories of Lidz and Lidz had a great influence on the practice of mental health professionals and implied parental responsibility for schizophrenia.

Lyman C. Wynne continued along the lines of theories of separation-individuation where unstable stretching of family boundaries of one member could lead to psychosis in another. The mode of communication in these families became to be called pseudomutuality, the unstable boundaries 'the rubber fence' (9).

The recommendation of psychoanalysis or intensive psychotherapy for the mother and long-term institutionalization for the schizophrenic child was made with great frequency, primarily on the basis of the theory that this would bring about the much desired separation–individuation and independence of the schizophrenic individual and his or her mother. The doctor–patient alignment prevailed with the assumption that the patient's improvement was facilitated by both the patient's and the therapist's rejecting the intrusive, over- or understimulating, over- or underprotective, critical, and engulfing family (that is, mother). The concept that the therapist was at the service of the patient and was his or her advocate against the destructive influences of the family became entrenched in the practice of psychiatry. Gradually, this evolved into studies of patterns prevailing in the families of schizophrenic patients.

FAMILY INSTITUTES AND PROJECTS: INTRAPSYCHIC, DYADIC AND TRIADIC FAMILY PATTERNS

In the 1960s a proliferation of family institutes and projects began: Some perpetuated the notion of villain and victim; others recognized the family as a resource for healing and as an institution committed to sound human connectedness in the midst of society's orientation to power, manipulation, competition, and acquisition.

The concept of the family as a source of healing was the underlying theoretical framework of Ivan Boszormenyi-Nagi of the family therapy project at the Eastern Pennsylvania Psychiatric Institute and of the Philadelphia Psychiatric Center's "Family treatment of schizophrenia in the home" project. The concept of the family as an institution committed to maintaining lasting human connectedness prevailed at Nathan Ackerman's Family Therapy Institute in New York.

The Family Therapy in Schizophrenia Project of the Medical Research Foundation, under the leadership of Gregory Bateson, Donald D. Jackson, Jay Haley, and John Weakland, dealt with family homeostasis and concepts of the double bind as a mode of communication in families with a schizophrenic member. The double-bind situation implies that the schizophrenic individual is involved in an intensive relationship with a person who gives messages that contradict each other and about which the schizophrenic individual is unable to comment (that is, he or she cannot make a metacommunicative statement.)

Psychiatry has subscribed for many decades to making a person as an individual the focus of study, with elaborate postulations of what transpires within the person and is transferred onto another. Given this heritage, it is not surprising that viewing patterns of families and other social systems as determinants of relationships and pathology meets with continued resistance. There has been a gradual move from pathological dyads to pathological triads; there has even been speculation that schizophrenia might be the manifestation of adapting to many conflicting triangles in a family. Jay Haley felt that a person could change only if the context of relationships in which he or she lived also changed. Jay Haley and Cloe Madanes created the strategic family therapy that had as its primary goal helping parents to regain a hierarchically dominant position and to use this position in demanding appropriate role function of the disturbed offspring. The goal here was again the much touted but often undesirable and ineffective separation of schizophrenic patients and their families.

The efforts to study patterns in families with a schizophrenic individual persisted, especially in the areas of communication deviance and marital discord. The tendency to fragmented and amorphous styles of conversation was studied by Singer, Wynn, Toohey, and others, who linked aspects of thought disorder to parental communications (10).

By the mid-1970s Reiss, Mischler, and Waxler studied marital discord in families with a schizophrenic offspring (11, 12). Extant areas of study were no longer perceived as the cause for schizophrenia. There was now documentation of parents' difficulty in jointly solving problems, a finding that is not uncommon among parents with a child whose development deviates from expectations of age norms and that is not necessarily unique to schizophrenia.

RESEARCH AND CLINICAL OBSERVATIONS

Researchers tell clinicians that their concepts, hypotheses, and theories are so imprecise and vague that they must be translated into other terms to be studied. Researchers say, "Who are we to judge whether expression of support, agreement, and positive regard are 'pseudo' or 'truly' mutual? How can we measure double binds, contradictory messages, and ways of metacommunication?"

Over the years, more rigorous research methods have evolved to distinguish families of schizophrenics from other families. While clinicians talked about dyads and triads, researchers talked about strategies of control and expressiveness.

Before new methods are accepted, old ones have to be shown to be ineffective. In the early 1970s, Henry N. Massie and Christian C. Beels showed that therapist alliance with the patient and its implicit blame on the family did not alleviate symptoms (1). Around the same time, Brown, Birley, and Wing were credited with discovering the now well-known high expressive emotion (EE) in a family member as the culprit for potential relapse in the schizophrenic family member (13). Anderson et al. view this as a response to the disorder as well as negative influence on it (14). It is crucial to pay attention to the reciprocity of these interactions. Research in mental health in which only one member of the family other than the patient is the subject of study can lead to harmful labeling of individuals, especially when the results of the research are applied clinically and taken out of context. Some clinicians have a tendency to drift toward rigid application of standardized procedures that, although useful for research, tend to be misapplied clinically.

In reviewing medical records of patients transferred from an acute-care setting to a state hospital I discovered the use of the phrase "the high EE mother" with a critical overtone similar to that applied to the "schizophrenogenic mother." The bridging of the gap between research findings and appropriate clinical application requires as much attention as the research itself.

PARTIAL HOSPITALIZATION: AN EXPERIENCE

In 1965, I was asked to develop a partial hospital as a federally mandated part of a Community Mental Health–Mental Retardation (CMHMR) Center. At that time, psychoanalysis was in its prime, CMHMR in its infancy. The partial hospital was called "Day Center Services," in an effort to reduce stigma and isolation for patients who attended. Minimal resources were available: inexperienced staff, space that no one else wanted and that had been condemned for nighttime use, county reimbursement of $24 per six hours per day per patient for 120 days a year, colleagues who were resistant for economic and other reasons to integrate the concept of partial hospitalization into options of treatment for their patients, and insurance companies who would not reimburse for partial hospital treatment.

In spite of these obstacles, this partial hospital rapidly expanded from three to 120 active patients, with development of a community satellite. The staff acquired expertise in creating an environment that prevented relapse and took pride in maintaining patients out of the hospital, thus fulfilling its mandate. Unlike in families, staff could be hired to fit the patient population, high EE staff moved on or were trained to become low EE. Low EE staff remained, and turnover was minimal.

What about the concept taught in residency training that patients who recovered in the hospital and were sent home to families relapsed and had to be readmitted? That would indeed defeat the purpose of the partial hospital. How could families, staff, and patients become partners in the endeavor to keep patients out of the hospital? The only limitation was time and money—no theoretical or research constraints existed, and minimal bureaucratic accountability had to be adhered to 20 years ago, in a setting unfamiliar to most theoreticians and researchers. Informal evening gatherings with refreshments were made available to families, followed by small group meetings that nowadays would be called psychoeducational in nature. Initiative and enthusiasm without tangible rewards only lasts for a humanly limited period of time, and it was found that daytime multifamily groups were more expedient in terms of staff time. Several of the family members had had many years of psychotherapy and contacts with the mental health system. There were families, especially single-parent families and disorganized families of the slums, who could not come to the family groups. In such cases, two staff members would go into the family's home at a time that all family members were home and offer a series of six to 10 psychoeducational family sessions. Use of staff time in this manner was feasible since initially patients attended from 9:00 a.m. to 3:00 p.m.

The rate of reimbursement for partial hospitalization in Allegheny County, Pittsburgh, Pennsylvania was not increased in the course of 20 years. More and more patients had to be seen; more and more prescriptions had to be written; fewer and fewer families could be seen. Research on the effectiveness of what transpired that might convince colleagues, legislatures, and insurance companies of the efficacy of partial hospital treatment could not be carried out because of lack of funds and research staff. As inflation increased but reimbursement did not, family contacts diminished. Families were seen on admission of the patient and at most twice a year thereafter or for crisis intervention, but not for crisis prevention. A booklet was designed to help families address salient issues:

HELP FOR THE FAMILY

What to do when mental illness strikes:

- DO share responsibilities with experts.
- DO find out who is well-informed and caring.
- DO consider the safety of yourself and the patient.
- DO read what you are asked to sign.
- DO consider other family members, their understanding and level of participation.
- DO give yourself credit for what you know, and share what you know with the mental health professional.
- DO learn about mental illness—acute, recurrent, and chronic symptoms; medications; side effects.
- DO learn about the nature, length, and cost of treatments (public and private).
- DO learn indicators of imminent crises and what precipitates them.
- DO help with medication compliance.
- DO share what you have learned with others who are not familiar with what you are experiencing.
- DO learn about respite care.
- DO learn about estate planning for incapacitated dependents.
- DO teach the mental health professional that *your* well-being is as important as the patient's welfare.
- DO find out about support groups from the National Alliance for the Mentally Ill, Washington, D.C.
- DO become an educated, articulate advocate.

DO NOTs:

- DO NOT shift responsibility from patient to family to mental health professional.
- DO NOT agree to hasty dispositions.
- DO NOT assume one mental illness is like another, one mental health professional like another, one medication like another.
- DO NOT set up an adversarial situation.
- DO NOT get drawn into unrealistic perceptions; do not argue with delusions.

DO NOT isolate yourself from the patient, your family, friends, co-workers, employers, and so forth.
DO NOT subject yourself or the patient to tasteless humor, teasing, and ridicule.

One of the policies of the partial hospital was to obtain all old records of a patient, review them thoroughly to avoid repetition of ineffective patterns of intervention, and learn about effective interventions for the patient. Effectiveness was defined as keeping the patient functioning in the community. In the course of these reviews, we learned about the attitudes (documented) of professionals with whom patients and families had been in contact over the past 10–30 years. More often than not we concluded that families needed a corrective emotional experience from professionals they had encountered in the course of their participation in the treatment of their schizophrenic relative (15).

CASE HISTORY
Changing Attitudes Over 30 Years

A.B. was referred to the partial hospital by a psychoanalyst who had seen the patient for 12 years. The reason for the transfer was that the psychoanalyst was moving out of town. However, the patient chose to perceive the situation as though he had sought the new therapist out himself in contrast to being made to see the previous psychiatrist by his parents. The patient was 33 years of age at the time of referral, and he and his family had been involved with community resources and educational and mental health systems since the patient was five years of age. These institutions included Johns Hopkins Institute and Clinic in Baltimore, Maryland, and the Child Guidance Center of Western Psychiatric Institute and Clinic in Pittsburgh, Pennsylvania. Though the family is Presbyterian, the patient, who was not kept at a university-affiliated school, was sent to Mt. Mercy Academy, Ursaline Academy, East End Lutheran School, and subsequently a private tutorial school, and finally Devereux School, Devon, Pennsylvania. The patient had been in St. Francis General Hospital (now St. Francis Medical Center) and Partial Hospital and also in recreational and work programs such as the Council House (now Renaissance Center) and the Vocational Rehabilitation Center in Pittsburgh. He saw physicians frequently and had workups at the Mayo Clinic for various somatic preoccupations. The patient had been variously diagnosed as mentally retarded, schizophrenic, behaviorally disturbed, and organically brain damaged.

His thought content ranged from grandiosity to lack of self-esteem to excessive preoccupation with bodily functions. His voice was booming, especially when he was excited; his gestures were poorly coordinated. He dressed in either unmatched, loudly colored clothing or in a very formal business suit, in which he pretended he was going to a downtown office. He responded well to instructions on how to dress more appropriately for the situation he was in. Initially he blamed his parents and the mental health system for his condition and the variety of diagnoses placed on him as well as his inability to obtain a higher education. He was quite articulate but frequently misused words. He wrote with a tremor and had difficulty with numbers. He had difficulty paying attention to significant details, but he could learn, although very slowly. He oscillated from overdepending on his parents and expecting them to tolerate any behavior from him as well as sponsor his every need, to wanting to be more autonomous than his basic limitations realistically allowed. He was interested in peer companionship and in dating, but opportunities were very limited, almost unavailable at his parents' rather comfortable socioeconomic level. The patient spent much time in bed, unable to structure his day.

In the records, the mother and paternal grandmother were described as having excess concern; for example, "although the family pediatrician kept reassuring mother, mother was constantly worried." From the records, it was readily apparent that mother had ample reason to be worried and that the pediatrician was not listening to her. (Unfortunately, these cases are generally not the ones that physicians follow up on, and the same mistake occurs over and over.) Generally, the caseworkers described the mother as suffering from personal feelings of inadequacy, loneliness, and isolation from her family. There was little substantiation of these observations. Critical comments about "her upper-middle class lifestyle" were recorded. Her absorbing interest in her son and genuine desire to take care of him as best and as long as she could was described more as a deviance than as an asset. The father was described as detached from the day-to-day problems the patient presented, but observant and concerned about the patient's slow development. The mother expressed slight discontent about the father having to be away so much on business. The father regretted not having more time for his son. The fact that this couple wanted a large family when conception took place only after 24 years of marriage was mentioned but not taken further into account in formulation of recommendations. The social worker commented in the records which were reviewed that treatment would not be effective and she would recommend schools. In the two lengthy diagnostic interviews with a child analyst, no comment was made about the patient's cognitive impairments. The only recommendation made was that "this boy and mother separate." Undoubtedly well versed in Margaret Mahler's theories of separation–individuation, the analyst, in applying it to this case, only created more pain and certainly resolved nothing. The mother valiantly continued to raise her son, who remained an only child. She devoted much time to attending to his specific needs, which included tutoring him in basic academic subjects when schools gave up. Her support system for doing this difficult task was minimal and consisted only of the individual therapy she continued for herself for many years. Diagnostic assessments were plentiful, but appropriate treatment plans were lacking for her son. Placement at Devereux School was recommended. He had to be sent away from home because of lack of appropriate resources near home. He perceives this as a rejection to this day. His reality testing remained precarious. The patient always related better to the staff than to other patients because he needed the structure the staff could provide for him. His mother laid the groundwork for his ability to relate to staff in this manner.

When the patient first came to the partial hospital in 1975, his mother, then age 60, had been once more left with the task to motivate the patient to get out of bed. Following a severe depressive episode that culminated in a suicidal gesture and required a brief hospitalization, the patient was discharged with a schedule of programs to go to in the community during each day of the week.

The father's retirement was a turning point not only in the father's life but also in the patient's life. He willingly undertook the task of getting his son to places he was expected to be at. With the father's help, the patient learned to have his own bank account and learned to write out checks and not overdraw his account. Because of the role stereotyping that prevailed within the family as well as the mental health system, it was never suggested to the mother that she could help the patient in these rather essential endeavors. Although the patient found menial tasks below his dignity and social status, he was able to get satisfaction from working five days a week in a greenhouse under supervision, with daily feedback on his work performance and some remuneration, until the greenhouse closed because of lack of subsidy. The patient is now seen for chemo- and psychotherapy six to 12 times a year. The father comes in during the last 15 minutes of each session. In the course of these sessions, father was able to give up his unrealistic expectation that his son seek competitive employment.

In order to reduce the patient's high anxiety level and subsequent boisterous and overbearing behavior, which is poorly tolerated in group settings, he is maintained on mesoridazine besylate (Serentil) 50 mg three times a day, benztropine mesylate (Cogentin) 1 mg once a day, and on his own insistence, imipramine (Tofranil) 75 mg before sleep. With his mother's help, although he and she are quite aware of the possibility of tardive dyskinesia, compliance with taking medication has considerably improved in the course of therapy.

The father has since passed away, and the patient has become a help to his mother, now in her 70s, in maintaining them both in the family home with the assistance of a home health aide. Arrangements have been made for the patient to live near cousins in another state should the mother pass away.

This case ($N = 1$) highlights

1. the need for extensive training in psychiatry of all physicians regardless of specialty;
2. the need for psychiatrists to be more alert to cognitive deficits;
3. the need for appropriate community supports and resources to address the patient's needs throughout the life cycle—childhood, adolescence, young adulthood, adulthood, middle age and aging—encompassing schooling, employment, recreation, socialization, and housing;
4. the need for all mental health professionals to be aware of family resources, value systems, and role identities.

Clinical Practice, Research, and Funding

Well-funded outcome studies have shown that the partnership of family, patient, clinician, and researcher leads to reduced frequency of relapses and greater medication compliance (13, 14). However, when families no longer wished to wait to have their needs met, self-support groups evolved and began to gain support in more and more communities (see Chapter 3). Because of lack of funds and adequate staff, community mental health centers have much difficulty responding to the obvious needs of schizophrenic patients and their families. In our partial hospital, staff and space were reduced while ever younger and more acutely ill patients and perplexed parents came for services.

Although it is still resisted by some private practitioners and insurance companies and not adequately funded by governmental agencies, giving families support and sharing expertise by educating families is growing in some institutional settings.

Leff et al. (16) focus on reducing EE. A unique approach by this group is that they educate family members about schizophrenia in their own homes. Their main goal is to reduce family members' criticism, reduce their expectations to more realistic levels, and clarify symptoms. Relatives meet in groups biweekly for nine months, during which time high EE relatives are encouraged to adopt low EE relatives' coping styles of more social distance from the patient.

Another group who aim to reduce EE and relapse rate are Falloon and Liberman (17). They do this by multifamily interaction, education, medication, social-skills training, and behavior therapy techniques to alter family communication dysfunction. Educational workshops are provided weekly for nine months and subsequently on a monthly basis. Multifamily groups are provided at the clinic for two years. Communication guidelines for families are basically those practiced in a therapeutic milieu. They include listening respectfully, emphasizing positive reactions, reducing criticism, and making direct, calm requests for behavior change.

Although our perspective on what a lifetime commitment to an adult schizophrenic child means for a family has become somewhat more realistic, funding to implement what we have learned lags behind.

Each outcome study needs to have an implementation component attached to it, so that funding does not end when the research is completed but rather continues to provide the clinical care needed when the study is over.

Families of schizophrenic patients have risen to the occasion and continue to organize, learn, and support each other and their schizophrenic child to reduce isolation and relapse. However, we must remember that burnout of professionals and families needs to be prevented by the availability of suitable emotional and financial supports for all concerned.

FUTURE DIRECTIONS

We continue to need well-funded partial hospitals, respite care, supervised living arrangements, and, above all, flexible, supervised employment for the schizophrenic person, who more often than not wants the dignity and opportunity for some kind of employment. The family, patient, and professional now know that the prognosis for the course of many schizophrenic persons can be markedly improved when a particular kind of tolerant, even-tempered environment is available.

Our practice of the 1980s is characterized by reliance on economic considerations, and this greatly hinders the quality of care we can provide. Professionals need families to help alter this situation, and vice versa.

On the brighter side, however, five medical centers—Cornell; the Medical College of Pennsylvania; University of California, San Francisco; Long Island Jewish–Hillside Medical Center; and Emory University—have been funded to study the efficacy of treatment strategies for managing schizophrenia to help prevent chronicity. These centers will continue to study reduced medication strategies, medication targeted to symptom exacerbation, as well as the effect of family management techniques.

In summary, thought as well as money must help to translate well-designed research protocols into individualized applicable practice once outcome studies have shown us how to improve the quality of care for both the schizophrenic patient and his or her family.

References

1. Massie HN, Beels CC: The outcome of the family treatment of schizophrenia. Schizophr Bull 6:24–37, 1972
2. Haley J: Family therapy. Int J Psychiatry 9:233–242, 1970–1971
3. Bowen M: A family concept of schizophrenia, in Etiology of Schizophrenia. New York, Basic Books, 1960
4. Bowen M: The use of family theory in clinical practice. Compr Psychiatry 7:345–373, 1966

5. McFarlane WR: Family Therapy in Schizophrenia. New York, Guilford Press, 1983

6. Lidz RW, Lidz T: The therapeutic considerations arising from the intense symbiotic needs of schizophrenic patients, in Psychotherapy With Schizophrenics. Edited by Brody B, Redlich FC. New York, International Universities Press, 1952

7. Fleck S, Lidz T, Cornelison AR, et al: Incestuous and homosexual problems, in Schizophrenia and the Family. Edited by Lidz T, Fleck S, Cornelison AR. New York, International Universities Press, 1965

8. Lidz T: The family, personality development and schizophrenia, in The Origins of Schizophrenia. Edited by Romano Y. The Hague, Excerpta Medical Foundation, 1967

9. Green JR, Framo J: Family Therapy: Major contributions. New York, International Universities Press, 1984

10. Singer MD, Wynne LC, Toohey ML: Communication disorder and the families of schizophrenics, in The Nature of Schizophrenia. Edited by Wynne LC, Cromwell RL, Mathysse S. New York, John Wiley and Sons, 1978

11. Reiss D: Individual thinking and family interaction, II, in Family Process and Schizophrenia. Edited by Mischler EG, Waxler NE. New York, Jason Aronson, 1975

12. Mischler EG, Waxler NE: Family Process and Schizophrenia. New York, Jason Aronson, 1975

13. Brown GW, Birley LT, Wing JK: Influence of family life on the course of schizophrenic disorders. Br J Psychiatry 121:241–258, 1972

14. Anderson CM, Hogarty G, Reiss DJ: Family treatment of adult schizophrenic patients: a psychoeducational approach. Schizophr Bull 6:490–505, 1980

15. Goldstein M: The chronic mentally ill: selected aspects of treatment, past and present; eight case reviews. Interaction 3:2, Summer 1980

16. Leff JP, Berkowitz R, Kuipers L: Intervention in families of schizophrenics and its effect on relapse rate, in Family Therapy in Schizophrenia. Edited by McFarlane WR. New York, Guilford Press, 1983

17. Falloon IRH, Liberman RP: Behavior family interventions in the management of chronic schizophrenia, in Family Therapy in Schizophrenia. Edited by McFarlane WR. New York, Guilford Press, 1983

2

Helping Families in a Schizophrenia Program

S. Charles Schulz, M.D.
Janae House, M.S.W.
Marsha B. Andrews, M.S.W.

2

Helping Families in a Schizophrenia Program

Impact of Schizophrenia Upon the Family

The extreme stress and chaotic life-style that families of a schizophrenic individual experience because of the patient's often irrational and bizarre behavior is not accurately perceived by many people, including mental health professionals. Also, the extent of stress that a person with psychosis causes for close family members has not been documented until recently. According to these recent studies, schizophrenia symptomatology and less-then-optimum adjustment adversely affect many aspects of family life (1–12). Family life was reported to be so painful that families evaluated schizophrenia as being a worse burden than other serious illnesses. Schizophrenia is described in these studies as causing such a tremendous change in all family members' lives that the resulting psychological misery and depression can be like prolonged grief that is never resolved. Families are troubled by the patient's unpredictability, irrational sense of logic, severe withdrawal, extreme apathy and inactivity, lack of motivation, lack of interest in virtually everything, inability to function during acute episodes, occasional violence, and suicide attempts. The degree of financial strain and dependence on the parents is great because most schizophrenic individuals are unable to fully support themselves. Many parents express rage and bitterness that more is not being done to give families some occasional respite from the daily care of their children (13, 14).

THE FAMILY AS AN IMPORTANT SOURCE OF TREATMENT IN SCHIZOPHRENIA

Social workers in the early 1900s recognized the family as an important treatment entity. Naturally, the family provides the nucleus of social relationships and exerts a great influence on behavior (15). Psychiatrists included the family into treatment modalities 40 years later, as recognition grew that patients could not be treated in isolation from such influential environmental factors as their family (16, 17). Research with families based on this so-called medical model proceeded parallel to dynamically oriented family interventions. This research has had significant influence on contemporary mental health by broadening the field's focus from the intrapsychic pathology of the individual patient to the family context as a significant influence on the problems of identified patients. Mental health practitioners have increasingly used a biopsychosocial treatment approach that includes the family without conceptualizing them as the primary focus or etiological agent.

The family has long been considered to be a causal factor in schizophrenia and hence an unusable treatment ally. Also, because the family was seen as part of the etiology of schizophrenia, family members rarely received appropriate sympathy and support. Research into the biological parameters of schizophrenia and the resulting belief that many of the symptoms of schizophrenia are caused by brain dysfunction has allowed mental health professionals to lift the burden of guilt from the family.

With the shift in public policy in the past 20 years toward deinstitutionalization of the chronically mentally ill, supervision of patients increasingly has fallen upon their families. For schizophrenics close to their families, the importance of the family is great. Family members often represent the patient's primary source of companionship, involvement in pleasant activities, and assistance in coping with day-to-day problems. Since a relationship between stress or perceived stress and the exacerbation of schizophrenic symptoms has been demonstrated, tension in the home and hostile, critical attitudes or markedly intrusive, emotionally overinvolved attitudes on the part of family members toward the patient can lead to significantly increased chances of relapse (18, 19). Vaughn and Leff (10) demonstrated that patients whose families were characterized by high "expressed emotion" (EE) have a 50 percent relapse rate in the first nine months after hospitalization, whereas the relapse rate is 13 percent for patients whose families are low EE. If families can be treated as allies and enhance the patient's treatment compliance with psychosocial interventions and drug therapy, relapses and rehospitalizations may be reduced (5, 20).

However, although numerous studies and clinical experiments with home-based treatment of mental illness have led mental health professionals to regard the expansion of services for families as essential to the process of successful deinstitutionalization (11, 18, 21–26), in general mental health care has been negligent in educating families about the nature of illnesses such as schizophrenia, in training them in specific skills that are important in long-term management of the mentally ill, and in providing them with emotional support. Most families are inadequately prepared, to say the least, to assume the role of caretaker of the schizophrenic family member. In many professional schools and among practicing mental health professionals, it remains taboo to discuss diagnosis, especially of schizophrenia, with either the patient or the patient's family. Such practices make it difficult to educate the patients and their families, much less prepare them for dealing with a chronic disabling illness.

GROUPS FOR FAMILIES OF SCHIZOPHRENIC PATIENTS

The concept of groups as a source of support and guidance for the relatives of handicapped and stigmatized populations is not new. The efficacy of group approaches to the problems of families is reflected in (a) the extensive literature on professionally led groups for the relatives of the physically handicapped and the mentally retarded (23, 27–33) and (b) the proliferation of self-help groups for members of families affected by divorce, widowhood, alcoholism, child battering, and sudden infant death syndrome (34). However, group psychotherapy as an intervention for families with a schizophrenic member has received comparatively little attention in the literature. Only through the convergence of such factors as the recognition of schizophrenia's impact on the family, the increased awareness of the biology of schizophrenia, and the findings from research on expressed emotion has family education as an intervention appeared.

Specialty Programs in Psychiatry

The Schizophrenia Program at the Medical College of Virginia has as its major goal the provision of comprehensive and continuous care to schizophrenia patients and their families. In addition, program staff focus their energies on the specific difficulties of schizophrenic patients.

As part of the Schizophrenia Program, a short-term group was formed for the relatives of patients in the program by the Department of Psychiatry at the Medical College of Virginia. The patients are entered in the Schizophrenia Program generally following discharge from the College's inpatient service, with the entrance criterion being a *DSM-III* (*Diagnostic and Statistical Manual of Mental Disorders* [*Third Edition*]) diagnosis of schizophrenia. Of the first 27 patients in the Schizophrenia Program, 17 were represented in the family group. The patients' ages ranged from 17 to 35, with the majority being in their mid-20s. Fourteen were male, 13 were female, one patient was married, and 13 lived with their parents. The length of time of illness varied from three years in the younger patients to 16 years. All patients had experienced multiple hospitalizations for schizophrenia, the fewest being two and the most being 17 admissions.

Three separate groups were used to keep the number of participants in each group between five and eight and thus maximize group work. Each group met for eight consecutive weeks for one and a half hours per session. The total number of participants completing eight sessions was 17. Of the 17, 12 were mothers, two were aunts, two were fathers, and one was a sister.

Families were invited to attend the group either because they had expressed a desire to know more about schizophrenia and its management or because a clinical assessment of the patient and family indicated a high risk for relapse (that is, existence of intrusive, hostile, or overinvolved behavior and excessive amount of face-to-face contact on daily basis). Two families refused the invitation to join the group, one because of job conflict and the other for lack of seeing a need for participation. Of the 15 families who attended, three failed to complete the group series: one because of personal illness, one because of new employment, and one because of lost transportation.

Family Group Curriculum

The group's purpose was twofold. First, the group was educational. Knowledge was a first priority—knowledge of the illness in layman's terms, with examples of symptoms and behaviors that all could identify. Families were informed of appropriate expectations and the availability of community resources. It has been shown that better morale of families is associated with their knowing that what they do makes a difference (15). Education was not limited to the illness but included communication skills and problem-solving techniques. Second, the group offered support to families in coping with behavior of the mentally ill. This was done by allowing expression of the feelings of isolation, frustration, and powerlessness that occur within these families (28, 35). Parent input in the group was valuable to other members in explaining the illness in jargon-free language, helping them to understand and accept their own attitudes, assisting them in locating services, and giving them ideas for daily behavioral management (21). The group leaders sought to increase the predictability and stability of the family environment by decreasing family members' anxiety about the patient and increasing their self-confidence, their knowledge about the illness, and their ability to react constructively to the patient. As an example, many family members were unaware of differences between medication side effects and emergence of new symptoms. By teaching the family appropriate management techniques for coping with schizophrenic symptomatology, we hoped to decrease the pressures placed upon the patient and diminish the possibility of overstimulation from some aspects of family life, particularly affectively charged communications that are characterized by criticism and/or overinvolvement.

The group organization was based upon a psychoeducational model derived from a synthesis of clinical experience and interdisciplinary research (36; see Appendix). The model chosen was straightforward and structured due to the assumption that a clear and directive "road map" would be effective. It was also supportive, concrete, and educational since the ambiguity present in most therapeutic situations seemed to be nonproductive and even counterproductive for those highly stressed families and patients and for the clinicians who were attempting to help them.

RESULTS

Of the 12 families who participated in the entire series of eight group sessions, all expressed strong approval of the group. Group members' enthusiasm was evident in the unanimity of signed evaluations when a signature was optional. Family members agreed that the group had increased their understanding of schizophrenia, and each felt varying degrees of lessened anxiety in living with and supervising their relative.

The group members were candid in their use of personal examples for the group discussions. The educative component was frequently based on the examples presented by group members. Members shared techniques that worked, as well as ones that did not. Through such sharing the group developed a supportive environment. This support gave many the strength to venture out of their self-imposed isolation. Several members began attending meetings of the local Schizophrenia Foundation, and two members referred friends to our clinic who have a schizophrenic family member. These examples, along with less dramatic but still major accomplishments (e.g., family going out for dinner, taking day trips, and so forth) portray the decreased feelings of isolation, lessened burden of guilt, and increased awareness of community resources that the group members experienced.

To illustrate, Mrs. H's son had been diagnosed as schizophrenic for 16 years. She had relieved him of all household responsibilities because he was "disabled." Through education about the nature of schizophrenia and support from the group, Mrs. H was able to develop a plan for her son to participate in household chores. She was able to set realistic goals and gradually increase levels of his involvement in the house without escalating expressed emotion. The group was her place to ventilate frustrations with the process but also her place to receive positive rewards when she announced her son had washed the dinner dishes.

Mrs. R provided the group with a story that encouraged other members to keep trying. Mrs. R's son had been schizophrenic since college (approximately 12 years). He frequently had broken into neighborhood houses because of delusional beliefs and would disappear for long periods of time. Mrs. R and her husband had not been able to deal matter-of-factly with their son even after he broke into their store and "cleaned up" for them by putting everything in garbage bags. After entering the

Schizophrenia Program, Mrs. R's son was able to live first in a supervised community home, then in his own apartment. Mrs. R was able to share with the group the anxieties as well as the rewards she felt in seeing her son living independently. He has been in his own apartment for more than one year.

A difficult part of the program to assess is whether families use problem-solving techniques. If nothing else, the group did raise members' awareness that situations might be handled more effectively and in a less emotionally charged tone. This is demonstrated by the fact that group members called each other and discussed situations before the emotional level escalated or the emergency room was contacted. Also, members reported on how they previously had coped with the schizophrenic family member's behavior and the varying outcomes. Prior to the group sessions, a call or report from these families meant rehospitalization was imminent. It is our impression that for families who attended the group, rehospitalization was avoided repeatedly. Another factor contributing to this phenomenon could be that the families' knowing the therapist better set up a more cooperative situation. The details of the problem could then be assessed more accurately and a plan devised so that the family felt supported.

Of the 17 patients represented in the family group, seven (41 percent) were rehospitalized in the one year postgroup period. Three of the seven were patients represented by the families who did not complete the group sessions. Of the other four patients, one chose to leave the Schizophrenia Program and three had exacerbations of symptoms. However, the hospital stay of one of these three was 21 days, when past hospitalizations had been six months and two years. The second patient's hospital course was two weeks, whereas all previous hospitalizations had been for two months and longer. The third patient had two brief (less than 14 days each) hospitalizations for restabilization.

Of the original 15 participating families, totaling 21 individuals, four individuals (from three families total) dropped out by the fourth session. All had substantial reasons for not being able to continue with the group. Each individual remains in contact with the clinic, and our hope is to include them in a future group.

Discussion

We conclude that a psychoeducational group program for families of schizophrenic patients is a worthwhile component of comprehensive care. Although we did not have a control group and our findings are based on retrospective impressions, our findings are comparable to those reported by Anderson et al. (37) and Falloon et al. (5).

The consumer family seemed pleased as assessed by self-report. Eighty two percent of the group participants felt at the end of eight sessions that they wanted more sessions. At this juncture, their requests were based on continuing "what if" speculations, generally about daily management of behavior. The request for more group sessions was also based on the sense of unity the group had developed and their wish to not lose the group support. In response, we stressed other resources in an effort to broaden the families' resource base.

In summary, a psychoeducational group for family members of schizophrenic patients seems to be an important facet of a schizophrenia program. The group focused on education, problem-solving strategies, a decrease in feelings of isolation and guilt, and a strengthened relationship with the program. Although the success of these first three groups is measured testimony, it is of such a uniform positive nature as to allow us to recommend this modality. Further work by our group continues to refine that intervention.

References

1. Brown GW, Birley JLT, Wing JK: Influences of family life on the course of schizophrenic disorders: a replication. Br J Psychiatry 121:241–258, 1972

2. Creer C, Wing J: Schizophrenia at Home. London, Institute of Psychiatry, 1974

3. Davis A, Dinity S, Pasamanick B: Schizophrenics in the New Custodial Community: Five Years After the Experiment. Columbus, Ohio, Ohio State University Press, 1974

4. Doll W: Family coping with the mentally ill: an unanticipated problem of deinstitutionalization. Hosp Community Psychiatry 27:183–185, 1976

5. Falloon I, Boyd J, McGill C, et al: Family management in the prevention of exacerbations of schizophrenia: a controlled study. N Engl J Med 306:1437–1440, 1982

6. Grad J, Sainsbury P: The effects that patients have on their families in a community care and a control psychiatric service: a two-year follow-up. Br J Psychiatry 114:265–278, 1968

7. Hatfield A: Psychological costs of schizophrenia to the family. Social Work 23:355–359, 1978

8. Hoening J, Hamilton M: The Desegregation of the Mentally Ill. London, Routledge and Kegan Paul, 1969

9. Kint M: Problems for families versus problem families. Schizophr Bull 3:355–356, 1977

10. Vaughn C, Leff J: The influence of family and social factors in the course of psychiatric illness. Br J Psychiatry 129:125–137, 1976

11. Weiner L, Becker A, Friedman T: Home Treatment: Spearhead of Community Psychiatry. Pittsburgh, University of Pittsburgh Press, 1967

12. Weiner J: Five-year outcome in early schizophrenia. Proceedings of the Royal Academy of Medicine 59:17–18, 1966

13. Hatfield A: Help-seeking behavior in families of schizophrenics. Am J Community Psychol 7:563–569, 1979

14. Schulz P, Schulz SC, Dibble E, et al: Patient and family attitudes about schizophrenia: implications for genetic counseling. Schizophr Bull 3:504–513, 1982

15. Skidmore R, Thackery M: Introduction to Social Work. New York, Meredith, 1964

16. Mosher L, Keith S: Research on the psychosocial treatment of schizophrenia: a summary report. Am J Psychiatry 135:623–631, 1979

17. Mosher L, Keith S: Psychosocial treatment: individual, group, family, and community support approaches. Special Report: Schizophrenia 127–158, 1980

18. Bassin J, Drovetta D: Parent outreach. Exceptional Parent 6:6–9, 1976

19. Leff J, Kuipers L, Gerkowitz R, et al: A controlled trial of social intervention in the families of schizophrenic patients. Br J Psychiatry 141:121–134, 1982

20. Boyd J, McGill C, Falloon I: Family participation in the community rehabilitation of schizophrenics. Hosp Community Psychiatry 32:629–632, 1981

21. Atwood N, Williams M: Group support for the families of the mentally ill. Schizophr Bull 4:415–423, 1978

22. Brown G, Bone M, Dalison B, et al: Schizophrenia and Social Care. London, Oxford University Press, 1966

23. Cantoni L: Family life education: a treatment modality. Child Welfare 54:685–664, 1975

24. Greenblatt M, Moore R, Albert R, et al: The Prevention of Hospitalization: Treatment Without Admission for Psychiatric Patients. New York, Grune and Stratton, 1963

25. McFarlane WR: Multiple family therapy in schizophrenia, in Fam-

ily Therapy in Schizophrenia. Edited by McFarlane WR. New York, Guilford Press, 1983

26. Rice E, Ekdahl M, Miller L: Children of Mentally Ill Parents: Problems of Child Care. New York, Behavioral Publications, 1971

27. Huberty D: Adapting to illness through family groups. Int J Psychiatry Med 5:231–241, 1974

28. Mandelbaum A, Wheeler M: The meaning of a defective child to parents. Social Casework 41:360–367, 1960

29. Milman D: Group therapy with parents: an approach to the rehabilitation of physically disabled children. J Pediatr 41:113–116, 1952

30. Murphy A, Pueschel S, Schneider J: Group work with parents of children with Down's syndrome. Social Casework 54:114–119, 1973

31. Olshansky S: Chronic sorrow: a response to having a mentally defective child. Social Casework 43:190–193, 1962

32. Pollack G: Case Material and Theory. New York, Spectrum Publications, 1975

33. Yates M, Lederer R: Small, short-term group meetings with parents of children with mongolism. Am J Ment Defic 65:467–472, 1961

34. Killilea M: Mutual help organizations: interpretations in the literature, in Support Systems and Mutual Help: Multidisciplinary Explanations. Edited by Caplan G, Killilea M. New York, Grune and Stratton, 1978

35. Anderson C: A psychoeducational program for families of patients with schizophrenia, in Family Therapy in Schizophrenia. Edited by McFarlane WR. New York, Guilford Press, 1983

36. Zelitch S: Helping the family cope: workshops for families of schizophrenics. Health Soc Work 5:47–52, 1980

37. Anderson C, Hogarty G, Reiss D: Family treatment of adult schizophrenia patients: a psychoeducational approach. Hosp Community Psychiatry 6:490–505, 1980

Appendix

Families of Schizophrenic Patients Group

Overall Goals of Group

1. Educate families about their relative's mental illness and treatment
2. Develop additional support systems for patients and their families
3. Decrease the feelings of isolation, frustration, and powerlessness often experienced by families of the mentally ill
4. Actively involve families in patient's treatment
5. Help families better manage the patient's behavior
6. Understand, use, and control "expressed emotion" within the family
7. Decrease the relapse rate of the patient

Purposes of Group

First Session

1. Help families relax and feel less threatened by the idea of a group, leaders, hospital setting, and each other
2. Discuss purposes, objectives, and format of group
3. Educate families about the services of the Schizophrenia Program
4. Help families identify their expectations of the group

Second Session

1. Help families better understand psychiatric terminology, functions and roles of professionals of various disciplines, and types of therapies
2. Help families better understand etiological theories of mental illness, particularly schizophrenia
3. Inform families about medication categories, purposes, and common side effects

Third Session

1. Help families identify and explore behavior management problems
2. Help families understand the behaviors of schizophrenic people
3. Help families examine how realistic their expectations of the patient's behavior are
4. Enhance problem-solving skills and begin development of mutual support in the group

Fourth Session

1. Continue to examine management problems
2. Work toward concrete solutions that will effect some change in either patient's behavior or relatives' way of viewing it
3. Encourage increased interaction and support within the group

Fifth Session

1. Help families examine and take initial steps toward increased individuation and disengagement from each other by expanding their activities and number of supports in their communities
2. Encourage and examine activities for patients and families to participate in together that are fun rather than stressful
3. Help relieve the guilt and deal with the stigma associated with having a mentally ill relative

Sixth and Seventh Sessions
Reserved for discussion of topics of concern to families and/or staff. Topics may include drug abuse, alcoholism, sexuality, homosexuality, finances, vocational and educational opportunities, and legal issues.

Eighth Session

1. Review workshops and discussion
2. Provide opportunity for evaluation and feedback
3. Answer final questions
4. Make suggestions for future groups

3

Mutual Support Groups for Families of the Mentally Ill

Ruth Drescher, M.S.W.

3

Mutual Support Groups for Families of the Mentally Ill

> When the history of schizophrenia is finally written there will be a chapter on heroes. Foremost will be the patients themselves who suffered the terrible ordeal, trying to sort out thoughts and feelings amidst their incredible cerebral cacophony of dopamine dysfunction. Just behind them, however, will come the families who had to pick up shattered dreams and carry on bravely. In twentieth-century literature there will be few groups who will match the courage and perseverance of these. (Foreword by E. Fuller Torrey) (1, p. 10)

This chapter describes United Mental Health's Mutual Support Group Project for Families of the Mentally Ill, which was partially funded by a federal grant from January 1983 through June

---

The Mutual Support Group Project for Families of the Mentally Ill referred to in this chapter was supported by Grant No. 90PD86520/01 from the Office of Human Development Services, U.S. Dept. of Health and Human Services.

The Epidemiological and Psychological Indicators of Chronic Schizophrenia Project was supported by The Psychotherapy Research Branch of the National Institute of Mental Health Grant No. MH–535247 at Western Psychiatric Institute and Clinic, Pittsburgh, Pennsylvania.

The author acknowledges the cooperation of David E. Farley in the preparation of the original proposal; Beverly A. Schlotterbeck as public information director; and C. Lynn Howland as intern to the Project. Most particularly, thanks are due to the family members whose involvement and commitment made this project a success.

1984. United Mental Health is a private nonprofit advocacy and education agency funded primarily by the United Way, and it is the Allegheny County, Pennsylvania, chapter of the National Mental Health Association. Specifically, this chapter describes the model that was developed to stimulate the formation and maintenance of support groups for families of the mentally ill in the Pittsburgh, Pennsylvania, area. Although the terms "mutual support" and "self-help" are for practical purposes interchangeable, the author's preference for "mutual support" or "support" is based on the connotation that members are of help to one another; "self-help" carries a slightly greater connotation of individual self-reliance.

The goal of this project was to reduce the pain and stress of mental illness for both patients and their families by making use of emerging knowledge about mutual support groups, natural support, and networks (2–5). The overall objective was to develop a systematic and cooperative approach to the formation and maintenance of mutual support groups for the families of the mentally ill. Efforts were concentrated on the community mental health system in Allegheny County.

Allegheny County, in which Pittsburgh is situated, has a mixed urban, suburban, and rural population of 1,426,147 (1980 census). In fiscal year 1981–1982, an estimated 915 psychiatric patients who were discharged from community inpatient units or partial hospitalization programs returned to their families. An additional 171 patients who were discharged from state hospitals returned to their families. Therefore, at the very minimum, 1,086 families in Allegheny County were caring for a severely mentally ill relative. This figure does not include families who do not use public services or families whose mentally ill relative has not been hospitalized. At the time the grant proposal was being prepared, an estimated 682 of the 3,410 patients who were hospitalized in Pennsylvania's Western Region were expected to return to family settings.

The development of support groups for families of the mentally ill has lagged behind similar group development for almost any other condition. Certainly, collaboration between families and professionals could not have been expected in the past: Clinicians traditionally viewed families as interfering with treatment, at the root of the problem, disinterested, and/or manipulative (6–8).

Probably the most noteworthy and dramatic moment in the movement of family support occurred in September 1979 in Madison, Wisconsin, when 300 representatives of 80 support groups came together to form the National Alliance for the Mentally Ill, an organization whose current membership is 25,000 families, with more than 430 affiliate groups (James W. Howe, President of NAMI; personal communication, July 1985).

The combination of cutbacks in funding for consultation/education programming, a thrust toward deinstitutionalization with inadequate community resources, increased acceptance of the biogenetic theories of the origin of mental illness, and an overall movement toward self-help and mutual support explains why this was the opportune time for mutual support groups for families of the mentally ill to evolve and flourish.

RATIONALE

The basis of this collaborative approach between the service provider and the families was the hypothesis that if both the system and the families could profit from this intervention, then inevitably, and most critically, so would the patient.

Benefits for Families

In addition to providing the elements that contribute to relief from despair, guilt, isolation, and helplessness (9), mutual support groups for families of the mentally ill have a number of benefits. In a group setting, families can learn about the nature of mental illness; about methods of coping with undesirable behavior; and how to help the mentally ill family member by monitoring medication, learning to predict and avoid crises, and thereby possibly reducing the incidence of hospitalization. Families can become more knowledgeable about symptoms that are a function of the illness as distinct from behaviors which may be responses to environmental stresses. Thus expectations for a mentally ill relative can be adjusted to be more realistic. Mutual support groups can become effective advocacy vehicles to plead the case for the mentally ill. Services for the retarded, for example, have improved markedly since the National Association for Retarded Citizens became a viable force. This group of parents had to combat some of the same guilt and stigma that face the parents and families of the mentally ill.

Benefits for Providers

To the extent that families' stress levels can be expected to be reduced through learning and sharing in the groups, it becomes less likely that they will require mental health services for themselves.

Regarding the patients, recent studies have suggested that those who receive appropriate support from their relatives have fewer relapses and suffer less severe symptoms (10). The learning and support that takes place in the support groups can help families relate to the patient more productively, thereby reducing, if not eliminating, hospital stays.

The support group can become a vehicle through which families and professionals can relate at levels different from that of the client–therapist relationship. Staff can be freed from answering the same questions from multiple families. Staff and families' perceptions of each other can change, and they can work collaboratively on behalf of the patient.

Benefits for Patients

Benefits to patients accrue de facto by the benefits to families and providers. When the family has an avenue to express the despair and frustration that may result from having a severely mentally ill relative, the patient may become the beneficiary of a more constructive relationship with his or her family (11).

Because members of the support group share information about behaviors that appear to work, families develop a larger repertory of behaviors vis-à-vis the patients, and hence improved interaction can occur.

As families learn about material benefits to which their mentally ill relative is entitled, they are often able to acquire those that previously seemed out of reach.

Finally, and perhaps most critically, when members of support groups reach the stage at which they are organized and motivated to effect systems changes, the mentally ill gain organized and knowledgeable advocates.

Recognition of these numerous benefits to all parties involved made it clear that the time had come for families and professionals to work together—for dialogue and collaboration to occur that would facilitate the well-being of the mentally ill and the increased comfort of their families. The development of mutual support groups was seen as a viable method for achieving this goal.

METHODOLOGY

Eliciting the Cooperation of Community Mental Health Centers

The first step in implementing the grant was to contact each one of the community mental health centers (CMHCs) in Allegheny County. Relevant materials were presented to the directors of these CMHCs to introduce them to the purposes of developing these groups. They were then invited to participate in or send a representative to the Network, a group that is described later in this chapter. The plan to develop a lecture series to kick off the formation of groups was presented, and input was invited from the Network as to what should be included in the lectures.

Allegheny County is divided into 10 catchment areas. Of those, three already had well-functioning support groups for families of the mentally ill at the beginning of the Project. Five others opted to participate in the program to begin new groups. Consequently, by the spring of 1983, eight CMHCs were involved in the Project. (See Appendix A for a description of the characteristics of these groups.)

Concerns of Community Mental Health Center Directors

Staff Time. All the CMHC directors expressed concern about the use of staff time and how it could be accounted for in the system used by the county office that disbursed their funds. There was no disagreement that these groups should be viewed differently from therapy groups and hence should not be charged for service. It took some negotiating with the county office to come up with creative ways of accounting for the staff time for reimbursement purposes, but that has now been resolved and even appears as a legitimate activity in the county's annual plan.

Confidentiality. Notifying families of clients about the beginning of support groups was obviously a necessary first step, but to some degree it raised concerns about confidentiality. Ultimately, this was handled in a variety of ways: In some instances, the confidentiality question was ignored. Letters simply offering information about the beginning of the group were mailed to clients' families. In other instances, signed release forms were obtained from clients giving the agency permission to notify family members. In still other instances, there was no direct contact. Information about the groups was not directed at individual families at all but was handled on a community-wide basis through posters and the placing of brochures (which had been produced by United Mental Health for each group) in waiting rooms and other appropriate places.

Internal Support. Two levels of support within a CMHC are necessary for these groups to provide optimum benefit.

First, obviously, it is necessary to have the administrator's support. Three factors tended to influence the administrators: 1) the acquisition of federal funds, which gave credibility to the Project; 2) respect for the judgment of their colleagues, most of whom clearly were committing themselves to the Project; and 3) their own observation (and discussion about it with their staff) that the need was there.

Second, it is vital to have the support of the clinical staff. This was sometimes more elusive. Some clinicians found it difficult to dislodge their attitude that the families were to blame for a client's illness. One support group countered this attitude by presenting itself at a staff meeting. The family leader is reported to have said to the group, "When you first see us, you probably see us at a high level of craziness. We come to you filled with guilt, rage, and frustration, and we are heartbroken. Also we've probably had some bad, or at best rude, treatment somewhere along the line. What we hope is that you'll get to know us when we get past some of those feelings, and when we can relate at a more productive level. Having the group allows us to move to that point."

The administrator of that CMHC reported to us, "I think they really heard her. I used to hear a lot of talk like 'That family is making my patient even more crazy—no wonder he isn't getting better—we've got to get him out of that house.' I don't hear much of that anymore. What I hear about now are ways the therapist is exploring to find the best resources with the family to help the patient, whether or not he lives at home."

Therefore, the staff member who has the role of coordinator of the family support group must have a certain level of status and respect within the CMHC to help lend credibility to the group. Katschnig, who works with family groups in Vienna states, "The experts who work with relatives can be understood as 'outposts' of the professional system who gain new experiences the professional system was never before able to obtain and who can pass what they learn on to their colleagues" (12, p. 492).

The Lecture Series

In April 1983, the Project staff met with representatives of the three existing groups as well as those who were working toward developing new ones. At this meeting, the Project staff presented its plan to begin developing groups by sponsoring a six-part lecture series at each local center. With adaptation on the basis of comments by the coordinators, the lecture series took its final shape.

In September 1983, the beginning lecture series was launched. It was presented in five community mental health centers. Lectures were held once a week for six weeks. The following topics were discussed:

Mental Illness: Its Causes and Treatment. Each CMHC was asked to select its own psychiatrist to make this presentation. It seemed to make most sense to maximize the educational impact of this session by giving families the opportunity to meet a consulting psychiatrist in their own catchment area.

The Community System of Care for the Mentally Ill. This session gave the CMHC an opportunity to explain to families how the system works and how to make the most productive use of it. Each CMHC used its own staff.

The next four sessions took the form of a traveling road show:

Commitment Laws and Procedures. This presentation was made by a mental health review officer, a court-appointed official in Pennsylvania who rules on all commitment and recommitment hearings.

Wills and Estate Planning. This lecture was presented by an attorney experienced in these matters with other disability groups.

The Role of the Family in Helping its Mentally Ill Relative. Staff members of the EPICS (Epidemiological and Psychological Indicators of Chronic Schizophrenia) Project provided this information.

Mutual Support Groups: What Can They Do For Me? This sixth and final session was presented by the Director of the Mutual Support Group Project, the Public Information Director for the Project, and a family member who was instrumental in forming the first support group in Allegheny County. This session focused on a) the major functions of support groups, such as sharing, education, and advocacy, and why these functions are helpful to families and their mentally ill relatives; b) stigma as a major negative force for families and how to combat it; and c) the personal experiences of a family member with her ill daughter, her motivation to start a group, and the progress of that group from its inception to the present—approximately four years.

The lecture series was held during September and October in 1983, and the lectures were well-received. The attendance varied from five persons in one catchment area with a very low socioeconomic profile to 95 persons attracted by a hospital-based CMHC that augmented the promotion efforts of United Mental Health. At the end of each session participants were asked to fill out a brief questionnaire. Responses were unequivocally positive. For example, in response to the question, "Overall, I would rate this session as ___," 266 persons (61 percent) responded "excellent," 162 (37 percent) responded "good," 11 (two percent) responded "fair," and only one individual responded "poor." There were a total of 440 responses to this particular question. In general, to all of the questions asked, there was a consistent preponderance of "excellents." More than 500 people attended these sessions.

Continuation of Support Groups

The plan, from the outset, was to use the lecture series to do two things: provide much-needed information for family members, and lay the foundation for ongoing groups.

In all five locations, this method of starting the group proved to be effective. All of the groups that were started by the lecture series are functioning at this time, March 1986, two and one-half years after the beginning of the lecture series. Most groups meet monthly, although one group meets biweekly. Their styles vary from being primarily educational (a speaker every month, with a short social period for sharing) to placing a heavier emphasis on support in that the meetings consist almost entirely of sharing.

The grant included an evaluation component. The results of research that examined effectiveness in light of variables such as burden, social support and social network, coping capacity, guilt, stigma, self-esteem, and so forth, are reported by Drs. Biegel and Yamatami in Chapter 4 of this monograph.

Advocacy. As stated earlier, the ultimate goal of the Mutual Support Groups Project was the development of a strong grass-roots advocacy group made up of family members.

Out of the support groups grew an independent county-wide organization called ADMIT (Advocates for the Mentally Ill in Transition). Furthermore, all of the support groups are enlisted by United Mental Health to support or defeat specific pieces of legislation and are encouraged to offer testimony at the catchment area, county, and state levels.

Status of the groups. At this point, all of the groups are fulfilling their roles in providing support and education for families as well as being involved with advocacy activities; increasing their memberships; and struggling with issues of leadership, program development, identity, autonomy, and how to deal with difficult members. They are also learning to cope with the inevitability of internal conflicts.

Just as the entire population cannot be politicized, not all support group members can be mobilized into activist positions. Some people truly seek support and comfort only, but the strong advocacy groups, such as ADMIT and United Mental Health, can channel the energies of those who seek to make systemic changes.

The Role of the Professional

A spectrum of staff involvement was seen in these groups, ranging from overinvolvement that stemmed from an unwillingness to relinquish control to near uninvolvement. Generally, however, staff did perform a brokering function, helping families to make the best use of the system, in addition to playing a constructive facilitator role.

The decision to design this project to involve professionals was based on some very practical considerations. First of all, the community mental health system contained staff who were trained in group skills. Second, the same system had a built-in potential group to draw from for membership. Third, the professionals could provide such necessary resources as meeting space, printing and mailing, and information and speakers.

Ultimately, families would be able to take care of these details, but initially, the energy required for these chores might not be present in family members who were hurting and partially immobilized by the trauma that accompanies the onset and course of a confusing and baffling illness.

As Dr. Goldstein spells out in Chapter 2, earlier theoretical frameworks that were based on notions of faulty parenting and damaging family communication patterns resulted in negative perceptions going in both directions between families and professionals.

Lenrow and Burch point out that a key to the successful working of professionals with mutual aid groups is a positive mutual perception:

> We argue that while interdependence of the participants is obvious in mutual aid, its importance in professional helping has been neglected, obscured or denied in most training or practice. Our argument holds that where professional helpers and their clients take seriously their interdependence, the professional–client relationship has much in common with mutual aid among lay people. In both cases the participants learn to collaborate as partners with different but equally important resources to contribute to their common task. We hypothesize that when professional helping has

> these qualities, professionals and lay people in mutual-aid networks can learn much from each other's experiences. (13, p. 234)

This positive perception becomes possible for professionals who subscribe to the teachings of Bernheim (14); Seeman (15); Torrey (16); Falloon et al. (17); and McFarlane (18). These professionals, who can believe that schizophrenia is the result of biochemical and physiological forces, are able to view the family much the same way a physician would view the family of a diabetic person—as a resource to help the patient manage the disease.

One can begin to hope that the idea that families and professionals are worlds apart (19) will become less and less asserted—that the professional's perception of the family as damaged and responsible for the illness and the family's perception of the professional as blaming, neglectful, and adversarial will become outdated.

The Project, which now includes 22 groups, has revealed a number of elements that are essential for the professional's involvement to be most beneficial to the group:

1. basic respect for the humanity and growth potential of family members
2. current knowledge of etiology and manifestations of acute and chronic mental illness
3. maturity that permits the professional to work in a partnership and not need to control and manage the group
4. a sense of humor
5. the ability to help families use the system to the benefit of the patient
6. belief in his or her own ability to be helpful
7. genuineness
8. the ability to shed the mantle of therapist

Yalom has identified empathy, genuineness, and unconditional regard as the key ingredients in effective therapy. He asserts that these qualities are equally important in support groups (20).

A few examples of the kinds of problems that can develop when these characteristics are not present will serve to exemplify their importance. The professional who uses the group to satisfy her or his own power needs, who forces decisions upon the group, who discourages leadership from emerging, and who tends to steal the limelight will cause problems to develop within the group. (If the group can survive this individual, it may in fact coalesce as a result of the struggle.)

Moreover, the professional who wants to form a group in order to get families to do what he or she thinks they *should* be doing to care for their mentally ill relative will not help create the warm and supportive atmosphere necessary for sharing among family members. The professional's frustration as motivators to form the group is likely to cause the families to feel chastised and punished.

Finally, the professional who withdraws from the group precipitously, with no gradation or explanation, will give the group the impression that they were either not worth the professional's time or were being punished for becoming vocal. This leaves the group feeling rejected and helpless.

The Network

Some universal concerns and anxieties surround the starting up of a support group for families of the mentally ill. For example, some of the group coordinators who undertook this role felt the need for either sharpened skills or additional support. It was decided, therefore, that the leaders of the support groups, whether they were family members or professionals, needed a support group of their own. This Network had begun even before the grant was awarded, but it was formalized as part of the Project. The Network continues to meet bimonthly with a loose agenda that allows time for sharing experiences and needs.

Gradually, the number of family members in the Network has increased as these individuals have assumed leadership roles. The members of the Network requested that it be continued after the grant period ended; this has been done. Now in its third year, the Network comprises 22 groups, representing some 400 families.

Because the Network was designed to function as a clearinghouse, information is disseminated through United Mental Health to all the groups. During the life of the grant, a quarterly newsletter was published, entitled "Grant News," that primarily carried items related to legislative and regulatory matters. Now communication takes the form of memoranda and includes news of individual groups, legislative alerts, invitations to relevant meetings, conferences, and so forth, as well as Network meeting notices and minutes. Another communication-related endeavor was the formation of an Editorial Materials Board for the purpose of producing a handbook for families.

As a culmination to the grant, a subcommittee of the Network held a convention entitled "We Are Not Alone: A Convention for Families of the Mentally Ill," which featured Jack Hinckley as keynote speaker, in April 1984. Three hundred persons attended. A second similar convention was held in October 1985, featuring E. Fuller Torrey as keynote speaker, at which there were close to 400 participants.

In addition to conventions, workshops are held by the Network. A workshop on coping skills, to be conducted by a clinician and a family member in various locations, is in the planning stages. Earlier workshops were held on the role of the professional, the support group as a resource to agencies and hospitals, group dynamics, and procedures for starting a support group.

A small group of family members representing the Network has begun to meet with the administration of the state hospitals to find ways in which they can improve communications.

The Network publishes a directory to all of the support groups in the area, which is distributed through mental health agencies and state hospitals. As new support groups start, they are welcomed into the Network. At the time of this writing, four new groups are expected to be included in the next directory. One worker in a partial hospitalization group recently said, "I attended a Network meeting with a colleague, and the support and interest which I felt in that group prompted me to get involved back at my agency. There is a wonderful feeling generated in the Network."

The Network provides a unique forum for group leadership—one in which concerns and hopes are shared. The feeling that their individual small groups are a part of something larger prevails among families and professionals alike.

CONCLUSION

What seemed like a dream four years ago is now a reality in southwestern Pennsylvania—families of the mentally ill have "come out of the closet," and they are finding hope, relief, and comradeship through support, education, and advocacy.

Through the support groups, the process of communication begins to be positive in both directions: Families teach professionals how to understand them, how to communicate with them, and how to make use of them as resources; professionals help families to make the best use of the system for their relatives.

The dissatisfaction that families have expressed with professionals in the past (21) is a reason *for* rather than *against* acquiring the involvement of professionals.

The service delivery system is learning that families are a valuable resource, and professionals are listening to them.

Finally, resources are scarce, time is limited, and knowledge about reducing family pain through support groups is available. We must use the knowledge we have to make the most of the resources at hand in the shortest possible time. The resources, of course, are the expertise of both the families and the professionals, the needs of the families, and the willingness of both groups to work together.

Useful addresses can be found in Appendix B.

References

1. Walsh M: Schizophrenia: Straight Talk for Families and Friends. New York, William Morrow, 1985

2. Silverman PR: Mutual Help Groups: Organization and Development. Beverly Hills, Sage Publications, 1980

3. Snowdon J: Self-help groups and schizophrenia. Aust NZ J Psychiatry 14:265–268, 1980

4. Raymond ME, Slaby AE, Lieb J: The Healing Alliance. New York, W.W. Norton, 1975

5. Gartner A, Reissman F: Self-Help in the Human Services. San Francisco, Jossey-Bass, 1977

6. Hatfield AB: Families as advocates for the mentally ill: a growing movement. Hosp Community Psychiatry 32:641–642, 1981

7. Hatfield AB: Self-help groups for families of the mentally ill. Social Work 26:408–413, 1981

8. Appleton W: Mistreatment of patients' families by psychiatrists. Am J Psychiatry 13:655–657, 1974

9. Willis MJ: The impact of schizophrenia on families: one mother's point of view. Schizophr Bull 8:617–619, 1982

10. Anderson CM, Hogarty GE, Reiss DJ: Family treatment of adult schizophrenic patients: a psycho-educational approach. Schizophr Bull 6:490–505, 1980

11. Shapiro RM, Possidente SM, Plum KC, et al: The evaluation of a support group for families of the chronic mentally ill. Psychiatr Q 55:236–241, 1983

12. Katschnig H, Konieczna T, Sint P: Helping the family to cope with schizophrenia: professionally supported self-help, in Psy-

chiatry: The State of the Art. Edited by Pichot P, Berner P, Wolf R, et al. New York, Plenum Press, 1985

13. Lenrow PB, Burch RW: Mutual aid and professional services: opposing or complementary? in Social Networks and Social Support. Edited by Gottlieb BH. Beverly Hills, CA, Sage Publications, 1981

14. Bernheim KF: Supportive family counseling. Schizophr Bull 8:634–641, 1982

15. Seeman MV, Littman S, Plummer E, et al: Living and Working With Schizophrenia. Toronto, University of Toronto Press, 1982

16. Torrey EF: Surviving Schizophrenia: A Family Manual. New York, Harper & Row, 1983

17. Falloon IRH, Boyd JL, McGill CW: Family Care of Schizophrenia: A Problem-Solving Approach to the Treatment of Mental Illness. New York, Guilford Press, 1984

18. McFarlane WR: Family Therapy in Schizophrenia. New York, Guilford Press, 1983

19. Hatfield AB: Therapists and families: worlds apart. Hosp Community Psychiatry 33:513, 1982

20. Yalom ID: The Theory and Practice of Group Psychotherapy. New York, Basic Books, 1975

21. Holden DF, Lewine RB: How families evaluate mental health professionals, resources, and effects of illness. Schizophr Bull 8:626–633, 1982

APPENDIX A

Table 1. Characteristics of 10 Support Groups for Families of the Mentally Ill in the Pittsburgh Area*

Group	Approximate Size	Frequency of Meetings (per month)	Autonomy	Number of Leaders Professional/ Nonprofessional
1	20	1	2	1/1
2	10	1	1	2/0
3	60	1	5	0/1
4	30	1	1	1/0
5	20	2	0	2/0
6	25	1	5	1/1
7	10	1	0	2/0
8	40	2	3	2/0
9	28	1	3	1/0
10	40	1	4	6/1

*1–5 scale: 1 = lowest, 5 = highest.
Adapted from charts prepared by C. Lynn Howland, Intern, Mutual Support Group Project for Families of the Mentally Ill, United Mental Health, Inc. April 1984

Table 2. Characteristics of 10 Support Groups for Families of the Mentally Ill in the Pittsburgh Area

Group	Degree of Agency Support Administration/Clinic*	Community Characteristics
1	5/4	middle class, suburban
2	4/2	wide range lower to upper class, suburban and semirural
3	N/A	middle to upper middle class, suburban
4	4/4	lower to upper middle class, suburban to semirural
5	1/1	mostly middle to upper class, urban and suburban
6	N/A	mostly middle class urban, suburban, and rural
7	3/1	low to middle class, suburban
8	4/2	mostly middle class suburban
9	4/3	mostly middle class urban and suburban
10	3/5	wide range, urban and suburban

*1–5 scale: 1 = lowest, 5 = highest.

Table 3. Characteristics of 10 Support Groups for Families of the Mentally Ill in the Pittsburgh Area

Group	Internal Communication	Dues	Social Time After Meeting	Advocacy Thrust*
1	NL	no	yes	4
2	none	no	yes	3
3	HL/NL	yes	yes	4
4	none	no	no	1
5	none	no	yes	2
6	none	no	yes	3
7	none	no	yes	1
8	NL	no	yes	5
9	PC/NL	yes	yes	2
10	none	yes	yes	3

NL = newsletter
HL = hotline
PC = phone chain
*1–5 scale: 1 = lowest, 5 = highest.

APPENDIX B

Addresses

National Alliance for the Mentally Ill
Suite 500
1901 North Fort Myer Drive
Arlington, Virginia 22209-1604
Telephone: (703) 524-7600

National Mental Health Association
1021 Prince Street
Alexandria, Virginia 22314
Telephone: (703) 684-7722

4

Self-Help Groups for Families of the Mentally Ill: Research Perspectives

David E. Biegel, Ph.D.
Hidenori Yamatani, Ph.D.

4

Self-Help Groups for Families of the Mentally Ill: Research Perspectives

There has been increasing professional attention focused in the last several years on the problems and burdens of family caregivers of physically and/or mentally impaired populations (1–4). Families of the mentally ill are one such caregiver group that suffers from a number of significant stresses and burdens (5–12).

Self-help groups, which have existed in the United States since the founding of the republic, are one approach in helping to meet the needs of families of the mentally ill. The number and variety of self-help groups have grown significantly in the last decade. This growth of self-help groups in general is reflected in a large increase in the number of self-help groups specifically for families of the mentally ill. Such groups have developed through the efforts of parents of the mentally ill and

An earlier version of this chapter was presented at the 138th Annual Meeting of the American Psychiatric Association, Dallas, Texas. Ruth Drescher, Marion Zucker Goldstein, Barbara Shore, Edward Sites, and Richard Wells are thanked for their helpful comments in reviewing a draft of this chapter.

The Mutual Support Group Project for Families of the Mentally Ill referred to in this chapter was supported in part by Grant No. 90PD86520/01 from the Office of Human Development Services, U.S. Dept. of Health and Human Services.

interested mental health professionals and through sponsorship by community agencies such as local mental health associations. This growth was reflected in the establishment in 1978 of the National Alliance for the Mentally Ill (NAMI), which serves as a national advocacy and support mechanism for families of the mentally ill. NAMI's membership, which has doubled during the last 12 months, now includes more than 430 local affiliate groups, with a combined total of 25,000 families (James W. Howe, President of NAMI; personal communication, July 1985).

Although some research has examined the effects of such groups on families of the mentally ill (13–16), there is much that we do not know about the *functioning* of these groups. In this chapter we examine the ways in which self-help groups help families of the mentally ill to face their stresses and burdens. Our concern is with understanding the self-help experience itself, what people expect and receive from self-help groups and what actually occurs in these groups, rather than with an examination of how self-help groups change individuals. Thus the following two issues are explored:

1. *Assessment of the self-help group experience*: What are the characteristics of individuals who join self-help groups for families of the mentally ill? Why do individuals join these groups? How satisfied are they with their group? What do they find most helpful about their group? What do they like best about the group? What do they like least?
2. *Help-giving activities and processes*: What help-giving activities and processes occur in these self-help groups?

First, a review of the prevalent burdens and stresses facing family care givers of the mentally ill will serve as a necessary backdrop.

ISSUES AND PROBLEMS OF FAMILIES OF THE MENTALLY ILL

Relatives of the mentally ill shoulder a significant amount of care-giving responsibilities, often with inadequate assistance from mental health and human service professionals and agencies. The burdens of such care giving are multiple and pervasive and often contribute to feelings of guilt, resentment, worry, grief, and depression. Several significant issues and problems that face care givers of the mentally ill are cited in the research and practice literature.

Managing Their Mentally Ill Relatives' Symptomatology and Behaviors

Families need practical management techniques for addressing some or all of the following patient symptoms: hallucinations, irrational or blocked thought content, suspiciousness, inappropriate affect, social withdrawal, isolation, unusual beliefs, and mood swings. Assistance is also required in managing intrusive and disturbing behaviors including unusual eating and sleeping habits, aggression toward self and others, deviant sexual behavior, and argumentativeness. Lamb (10) noted that part of the difficulty facing families is that the patient behavior is often unpredictable and that families never know how a particular situation will affect a patient at a particular time. Patient reactions may sometimes include violent behavior. Spaniol and Jung conducted a national survey of members of self-help groups affiliated with NAMI (Report by the Center for Rehabilitation Research and Training in Mental Health, Boston University, 1983). They noted that families cite the management of disturbing behavior as the most frequent reason for rehospitalization.

Isolation of Caregivers of the Mentally Ill Due in Part to the "Stigma" of Mental Illness

Leff (12) noted that family caregivers lack intimate relationships that can be tapped for emotional support. Family members often feel a sense of shame or guilt, in part because of feelings of self-blame and in part because the patient's condition carries a stigma. These feelings may cause them to withdraw from others in their social circle. In addition, the patient's behavior may cause relatives and friends to avoid visiting the household or discussing the emotional difficulties the caregiver may be facing. The net result is that when family caregivers most need others for social support, there are few, if any, individuals available.

Interference with Personal Needs of Family Members

Families report that providing care for a mentally ill family member disrupts family life and may cause strained family relationships (particularly among siblings), financial hardship, neglect of personal needs, lack of leisure time, and stress-related health problems. Lamb (10) noted the all-encompassing nature of the burden of providing care for a mentally ill relative and suggested that even leaving the house to do some light shopping requires making arrangements for someone to watch the patient. As Lamb noted, "The relatives may not only become the jailers, but, in effect, be in jail themselves" (p. 92).

Inability of the Patient to Carry Out the Tasks of Daily Living

Patients may be unable to take responsibility for their own grooming and hygienic functions or to perform their share of household tasks. The latter may be more of a problem in low socioeconomic status households that are unable to pay others for the performance of these tasks.

Proper Use of Medication

The patient's adherence to a medication regimen is a major concern of families. Spaniol and Jung found that drug management is a key need of families and that monitoring of medication is inadequate and infrequent. In their national study of members of self-help groups for the mentally ill, drug medication was cited as an area of treatment needing the most improvement, with more than half the respondents (52 percent) being dissatisfied with medication services.

Mental Health Professionals Are Often Seen as Not Helpful

Family members complain that they have insufficient knowledge and information about mental illness—its treatment, availability of services, and practical management techniques. For example, Holden and Lewine (16) found that 32 percent of relatives of the mentally ill were given a diagnosis from 2–11 years after the initial breakdown. Even when families actively seek information, they rarely receive it in sufficient quality or quantity. For example, in a study by Hatfield (9), families of the mentally ill complained that mental health professionals only offered insight-oriented therapy; they did not give families what they wanted, which was a clear explanation of the patient's illness, practical help concerning how to handle patient behavior, and referral to appropriate community resources.

In fact, families often find other sources of assistance more effective than the help of professionals. Hatfield (14) found that families rated professional help much less positively than the help of parents of other schizophrenics, self-help groups, or friends and relatives. Spaniol and Jung asked respondents in their survey to report the level of satisfaction or dissatisfaction with seven professional activities: practical advice, information about illness, emotional support, referral, treatment coordination, attitude toward the family, and attitude toward the ill member. The most frequently occurring response was "very dissatisfied" for the first five activities listed above. Similar to the Hatfield finding, Spaniol and Jung reported that one-third of the sample (32.6 percent) felt the self-help group was their most important source of support, compared with one-fifth (19.6 percent) of the sample who cited mental health professionals as their most important source of support. Similarly, self-help groups are cited to a greater degree than are mental health professionals as most helpful in providing information.

METHOD

This research was carried out as part of the Mutual Support Group Project for Families of the Mentally Ill conducted by United Mental Health in Pittsburgh, Pennsylvania. The purpose of this project was to stimulate the development of self-help groups for families of the mentally ill. When the project began, three such self-help groups were already in existence in Allegheny County; an additional 11 such groups have been organized through the auspices of the project (see Chapter 3 of this monograph). The research consisted of two major components:

Treatment Survey

This study utilized the Pretest–Posttest Nonequivalent Groups Design (17). The term "treatment" is not being used in a clinical sense but rather as a research term to denote the group that received an intervention, in this case, participation in a self-help group. All new members of preexisting and newly formed self-help groups were asked to complete a questionnaire upon joining the group and again six months later. The questionnaire took approximately 30 minutes to complete and consisted of seven sections containing approximately 110 questions. Variables included: patient and caretaker characteristics, demographic and socioeconomic characteristics, patient's psychiatric history and status, caretaker burden, social network and social support, coping skills, self-esteem and relationships with mental health professionals. Completed questionnaires were received from 54 individual members of 10 self-help groups of families of the mentally ill. Of this group, 83 percent or 45 individuals also completed the follow-up questionnaire administered after six months' participation in the self-help group.

A comparison group of caretakers of the mentally ill who

were not members of a self-help group for the mentally ill was also included in this study. Three community mental health centers agreed to supply names for this group. Twenty-five completed questionnaires were received at Time 1 (T1) and 84 percent or 21 individuals also completed the T2 questionnaire. It was hoped that the comparison group would be large enough to allow matching with the self-help group. The sample size did not allow this. Examination of the comparison group characteristics showed major differences between the comparison and treatment groups pertaining to familial relationship of caregiver to patient, patient diagnosis, and length of patient's illness. Because of these differences, the comparison group was not used for data analysis.

Case Study

As a complement to the objective and primarily close-ended questions of the self-administered questionnaire, qualitative and open-ended interviews were conducted with five members of each of four self-help groups. Interviewees, who had been members of a self-help group for an average of two years prior to the interview, were selected nonrandomly by the group coordinator (in most cases a staff person) to represent a cross section of the group. The interviews focused on caregiver stress, organizational issues pertaining to the group, and members' perception of the strengths and weaknesses of their group. Case study interviews were conducted by C. Lynn Howland, M.S.W., and case study data was coded by Deborah Whitely, M.S.W.

DESCRIPTION OF THE STUDY SAMPLES

Caregivers—Treatment Group (*N* = 45)

Overall, caregivers represented a white, female, middle-class professional and semiprofessional group. More than one-half (63 percent) of the caregivers were parents of the patient, with

14 percent being a sibling and nine percent a spouse. Almost all (95 percent) of the caregivers were white and more than two-thirds (73 percent) were female. Most caregivers (71 percent) were married; one-fifth (21 percent) was separated or divorced, and the remaining eight percent were single or widowed. Caregivers ranged in age from 28–71 years, with the mean age being 51 years. Caregivers (or spouses, in the case of caregivers who did not work) were employed primarily in white-collar occupations (73 percent), with approximately one-fourth (27 percent) of the sample employed in blue-collar occupations. The caregivers were a highly educated group, with 95 percent being at least a high school graduate and almost one fifth (18 percent) being a college graduate. More than half (56 percent) of the total family incomes of the caregivers were greater than $20,000 per year; only 15 percent of the caregivers had annual incomes of less than $11,000 per year. The median income of the caregivers was above the national median family income level. Almost one-third (29 percent) of the caregivers belonged to more than one self-help group.

Caregivers—Case Study Group (N = 20)

The case study group, although very similar to the treatment group, differed on several variables. This group was more female (90 percent), slightly less white (90 percent), slightly older (mean age of 57 years), were often married (75 percent), and had higher educational levels (25 percent were college graduates). Income levels of the two groups were very similar, with a slightly larger number (22 percent) of the case study caregivers having incomes of less than $11,000 per year.

Patients—Treatment Group

Mentally ill relatives of self-help group members ranged in age from 19–70 years, with a mean age of 36 years. More than half (61 percent) were male and 39 percent were female. Schizophrenia was the most common diagnosis, with approximately one-half of the caregivers classifying their patients this way. Most patients had been diagnosed as mentally ill at least two years ago. More than one-half (59 percent) had been ill for more than five years, with almost one-third (29 percent) having been ill for more than 10 years. Most patients (84 percent) were unemployed; 9.1 percent were employed, and 4.5 percent were students. The patients were slightly less well educated than were their family caregivers: 15.9 percent did not graduate from high school, while the same percentage were college graduates. Almost one-half (48 percent) of the patients lived with their primary family caregiver, 18 percent lived in their own apartments, seven percent were in the hospital, five percent lived in a group home, and 22 percent had a variety of other living arrangements. More than one-third (39 percent) of the patients were hospitalized during the study period. Those who were spent an average of 82 days in the hospital, with an average last length of stay of 66 days.

Patients—Case Study Group

Patients of the case study group, although similar to patients of the treatment group, tended to be younger (29 years mean age) and in more cases were male (90 percent) and employed (35 percent). The levels of education of the two groups were identical. Almost two-thirds (65 percent) of the case study patients were diagnosed as schizophrenic and had been ill for slightly longer periods of time than had the treatment group patients (65 percent had been ill for more than five years, 35 percent for more than 10 years). Fewer (30 percent) of the case study patients were hospitalized, but they spent longer periods in the hospital (92 total days in the hospital and 92 days average last length of stay). A slightly lower percentage (45 percent) lived with their family caretaker, 20 percent lived in their own apartment, 15 percent lived in a group home, 10 percent were in a hospital, and 10 percent had other living arrangements.

FINDINGS

Treatment group caregivers were administered the 25-item Family Distress Scale by Pasaminick (18). As can be seen by examining the T1 means, the greatest burdens were worry about the patient's overall behavior, strain caused by the patient's being too dependent on the caregiver, physical strain, restlessness of patient, and the patient's requiring excessive attention from the caregiver.

Further insight on how caregivers feel about these burdens can be gained through an examination of the open-ended responses of the case study caregiver group. Caregivers discussed

Table 1. Caregiver Burden (Family Distress Scale)

Item	T1 Mean
1. Trouble at night	2.08
2. Nursing problem	1.06
3. Patient's safety	2.29
4. Patient's behavior	1.84
5. Patient uncooperative	2.23
6. Patient strain too dependent	2.67
7. Restlessness	2.49
8. Body complaints	2.36
9. Rude behavior	1.76
10. Odd behavior	2.43
11. Refusal to take medication	2.31
12. Trouble with neighbors	1.19
13. Household routine upset	2.23
14. Social or leisure interference	2.21
15. Stay away from work	1.40
16. Stay away from school	1.18
17. Overall behavior worry	2.81
18. Physical strain	2.50
19. Excessive attention	2.44
20. Children ashamed	1.61
21. Children afraid	1.55
22. Do you feel ashamed?	1.43
23. Are you afraid?	1.52
24. Do you feel embarrassed?	1.49
25. Do you feel guilty?	2.00
Overall scale mean	2.04

1 = "not at all;" 4 = "almost always"

burden in terms of emotional strains, its effect on family life, and frustration with the mental health system. By far, most responses addressed the issue of emotional burden. Respondents expressed feelings of frustration, and anger, and often bitterness toward their situation and their mentally ill relative. Caregivers described the burden as "continuous, always there, overwhelming." One caregiver remarked, "It's a little like being on a merry-go-round, you want to get off, but instead you start going back." A number of respondents discussed burdens in terms of disruption of family life. One respondent remarked, "The tragedy is the loss of the ability for feelings and relationships—the inability to love and be loved. This is a big, big loss for everyone. You even lose contact with your extended family."

Self-Help Group Experience

Caregivers were asked why they joined the self-help group, how satisfied they were with their group, and what they liked best and least about their group, and were asked to rate the helpfulness of the self-help group in seven different areas (see Table 2). The major reasons given by treatment group caregivers for joining the self-help group were related to enhanced social support: sharing experiences and interacting with others in the same situation (30 percent), gaining advice and information (25 percent), and obtaining help in coping (23 percent). (The remaining one-fifth of the sample gave a variety of other reasons

Table 2. Helpfulness of Support Group

Item	Mean
Helpful in caring for patient	1.98
Helpful in relationship with patient	1.98
Helpful with mental health professionals	1.98
Helpful with mental health system	1.90
Group advocate for better mental health	1.54
Group source of emotional support	1.61
Group source of education and information	1.41

1 = "very helpful;" 4 = "not helpful at all."

for joining the self-help group). Case study respondents expressed similar reasons for joining the self-help group. Typical comments were "frustration of not knowing where to turn, no private person to talk to . . . no one was there for our need" and "Something very devastating was happening to me and I needed something. The article I read gave me some hope." Other reasons given by case study participants for joining the group included positive experiences with counseling and/or other self-help groups and the suggestion by a mental health professional that they join a self-help group.

Treatment group respondents reported high satisfaction with their group: 42 percent were very satisfied, 44 percent were moderately satisfied, and 14 percent were neither satisfied nor dissatisfied. No respondents were dissatisfied. A slightly lower percentage (75 percent) of the case study group reported satisfaction with the group. One-fifth (20 percent) reported dissatisfaction, related not to the group per se but to their inability to become more active with the group because of work or family responsibilities.

Almost two-thirds (63 percent) of the treatment group respondents reported that sharing experiences and interacting with others in the same situation was what they liked best about the self-help group. Other reasons included the provision of empathy (28 percent) and receiving of information (10 percent). Case study participants reported similar feelings. Comments included "The other group members want so badly to lighten your load. You can be very open" and "Seeing the people and knowing they are the same as me. We all have something in common. We all share and we all benefit from each other's experiences." The aspect of self-help groups that was liked the least by treatment group and case study respondents related to organizational and membership issues (50 percent), with 17 percent of the treatment group respondents and 39 percent of the case study respondents not reporting anything as liked least. Other issues cited as problematic by a few treatment group members included frustration, repetition of the same problem, boredom, impersonalness, and lack of direct advice.

As can be seen in Table 2, the components of the self-help group reported as most helpful by the treatment group were its being a source of education and information, an advocate for better mental health, and a source of emotional support. The first and third components are certainly consistent with the reasons why individuals joined a self-help group, and with what they liked best about their group. It can be hypothesized that although advocacy was not an initial reason for joining a self-help group or was not what respondents liked the best about their group, it became important to participants because it represented one way caregivers could gain some control over chronic problems and issues. Similarly, it can be hypothesized that respondents saw the self-help group as less helpful (though still helpful) in their caring for and their relationship with their mentally ill relative and with mental health professionals and the mental health system because the self-help group could not be expected to have a direct impact on these issues.

In order to examine the possible variances in ratings of the helpfulness of the self-help group experience, overall helpfulness was further tested for association with a number of other major factors—functioning of patients, demographic characteristics of patients and caregivers, caregiver characteristics, and degree of program participation. The overall helpfulness of the self-help group experience was a composite measure based on the seven questions reported in Table 2, with a Cronbach's reliability rating of 0.83.

Helpfulness and Functioning of Patients

The functioning of patients was measured through 10 different variables: length of illness, hospitalization six months prior to the T1 and the T2 measurements, hospitalization in the last 12 months, number of times hospitalized prior to T1 and T2, number of times hospitalized in the last 12 months, total days in hospital at T1 and T2, and total days in hospital in the last 12 months. Of these variables, three relating to hospitalization of the patient were statistically related to the degree of helpfulness of the program: number of times hospitalized at T1, number of times hospitalized in the past 12 months, and total days in the hospital during the past 12 months. The magnitude of hospitalization was negatively related ($p < 0.05$) to the helpfulness variable such that the higher the number of hospitalizations and the higher the number of total days in the hospital, the less helpful the group participation.

In addition, the number of hospitalizations was tested for a pattern of association with each individual item represented in the overall helpfulness variable. The results showed significant relationships, again in the negative direction, for four out of seven variables, including less helpfulness with mental health professionals, the mental health system, as a source of emotional support, and as a source of educational information. There were no significant statistical relationships with helpfulness in caring for the patient, relationship with the patient, or the group as advocate for better mental health.

Total number of days in hospital during the past year was also further examined with each item representing the helpfulness variable. Only one of the items—helpful as provider of emotional support—was significantly related to the variable, again in a negative direction. The other remaining variables were related, though not statistically significant, in a negative direction—more days in the hospital, the less helpful.

These data suggest that when patients are in the most unstabilized phase of their illness, the problems facing the caregivers may be so great as to render the self-help group less effective in addressing their burdens. Self-help group members whose family members have experienced high levels of hospitalization may feel very pessimistic about the prognosis for their family member and may feel there is not much the self-help group can do for them at this juncture.

Helpfulness and Patient and Caregiver Characteristics

Patient demographics consisted of age and gender of patients; caregiver demographics included gender, marital status, educational level, type of occupation, and income level. None of these variables were statistically related to the overall helpfulness variable, indicating an even distribution of the degree of helpfulness among the selected demographic factors of patients and caregivers.

The major characteristics of caregivers were whether the participant was the primary caregiver, his or her relationship to the patient (parent, sibling, or spouse, for example), and whether the patient was living with him or her. As found with the demographic factors, none of these variables were statistically related to the degree of helpfulness of the self-help groups.

Helpfulness and Group Participation

A positive statistical relationship existed between the rate of program participation and helpfulness: The higher the group participation, the higher the helpfulness rating. Further examination with each of the items representing helpfulness revealed that the rate of program participation was statistically related to four out of the seven individual variables, including caring for the patient, emotional support, helpful with mental health professionals, and helpful with the mental health system. The remaining items were not significant at the 0.05 level but were associated with the participation rate in the positive direction. These findings were as expected: Respondents who get what they want and need from the group are likely to attend more often than less satisfied individuals.

To an extent, the large number of nonsignificant statistical relationships between the helpfulness variable and other possible predictor or intervening variables may be due to a fairly consistent high rating of helpfulness of the program by all study participants. The skewed positive and narrow distribution in the variable allowed a limited possibility for obtaining statistically significant relationships with other major variables that might have been relevant and meaningful for further explanation or qualification of the extent of helpfulness. Thus, we face the interesting quandary that the participants' very positive response as to the helpfulness of the self-help group experience, which by itself is an important indicator of the effectiveness of these groups, limits our ability to learn further whether the self-help group experience may be more effective for particular respondents.

The case study participants were asked to report the effects of self-help participation upon them. Respondents reported that the group helped them cope with the problem with greater confidence (50 percent) and talk openly about problems (27 percent). Some of the participants' statements are: "I am more able to cope, I know there is help out there. I know I have friends I can count on in the support groups"; "I am able to accept the illness better. I am able to talk more about it"; "It helped me to be more open with other people." One-fifth (18 percent) of the responses focused on increased information about the illness, which brings greater understanding of the problem and therefore allows one to cope better. Typical responses were: "I feel more knowledgeable. I learned there is no quick cure, rather how to live with it" and "Knowledge includes learning about the mental health system, understanding that many people have problems, and learning more alternatives." A small number of respondents (five percent) stated that the group helped to improve family relations.

The self-help groups also helped respondents to cope with burdens and strains. More than half (55 percent) the respondents indicated that the combination of emotional support (sharing feelings, help in accepting the illness) and information (speakers, films, and so forth) provided significant help in addressing their difficulties. A statement by one respondent sums it up very well: "The group is very helpful in sharing the grief and sorrow."

Help-Giving Activities in Self-Help Groups

Treatment group caregivers were given Levy's (19) 27-item scale of help-giving activities in self-help groups. The scale is based on a qualitative analysis of the processes thought to be operating in self-help groups. The behavioral definitions and the treatment group caregivers sample means for each help-giving activity are presented in Table 3. Only descriptions of the helping activities, and not the behavioral definitions, appeared in the questionnaire issued to the treatment group caregivers. Respondents rated the frequency of occurrence of each activity on a four-point scale from "never" (1) to "always" (4).

The most frequently occurring activities were Catharsis, Explanation, Empathy, Normalization, Mutual Affirmation, Encouragement of Sharing, and Behavioral Prescription. The least frequently occurring activities were Behavioral Rehearsal, Punishment, Extinction, Confrontation, Requesting Feedback, Of-

Table 3. Treatment Group Caregivers' Ratings of Frequency of Help-Giving Activities

Item	Mean
1. Behavioral prescription	2.6
2. Behavioral proscription	2.2
3. Behavioral rehearsal	1.4
4. Positive reinforcement	1.8
5. Punishment	1.0
6. Extinction	1.4
7. Modeling	2.1
8. Self-disclosure	2.3
9. Sharing	2.5
10. Confrontation	1.2
11. Encouragement of sharing	2.8
12. Reflection and paraphrase	2.1
13. Requesting feedback	1.3
14. Offering feedback	1.4
15. Reassurance of competence	2.2
16. Justification	2.4
17. Mutual affirmation	2.8
18. Empathy	3.2
19. Normalization	2.6
20. Morale building	2.3
21. Personal goal setting	2.1
22. Establishing group's goals	2.3
23. Reference to group's norms	1.3
24. Functional analysis	2.4
25. Discrimination training	2.1
26. Explanation	2.6
27. Catharsis	2.8

1 = "never"; 4 = "always"

fering Feedback, and Reference to Group Norms. These findings are very similar to Levy's analysis of the same scale used with a sample of 67 respondents from eight behavior control and stress coping groups and also are similar to the data reported above on what respondents receive from self-help group participation. The most frequently occurring activities are those that relate to social support—emotional, affirmational, and informational components of such support. Although samples in both studies were small, the data suggest that self-help groups have a common helping focus regardless of problem area or whether the groups' members are victims themselves or caretakers of victims. Further research is needed to test this hypothesis. These findings are also similar to client ratings of the most helpful characteristics of professional helping relationships as reported by Shulman (20). Shulman conducted a study of 1,000 child welfare and foster parent clients. Twenty-seven worker skills (qualities) were described. Respondents were asked to rate which worker skills were most important to establishing the helping relationship and which were most helpful in relation to the actual help received. Such helpful activities as sharing, empathy, and explanation were the most highly rated as helpful. These are very similar to the activities most frequently reported by the present self-help group participants. It should be noted that the present study measured frequency and not helpfulness, whereas Shulman's study measured helpfulness but not frequency. Nevertheless, the similarity of findings suggests, as Carkhuff (22) hypothesized, that a core of facilitative qualities underlies both professional and self-help relationships. Other research (21, 22) has suggested a common set of facilitative qualities that promote effective interpersonal relationships. Again, many of these qualities are related to the self-help group activities rated as most frequently occurring in the present study.

The most infrequently occurring activities, by contrast, tend to be more threatening, directive, structured, and focused on behavioral change. Although families of the mentally ill may require assistance in altering patterns of behavior and interaction with their mentally ill patient and in learning specific skills for coping with this chronic problem, they are unlikely to receive such assistance through their self-help group. Of course, self-help groups are just one mechanism to help meet needs of families of the mentally ill. Professional assistance to families through structured educational and counseling activities may also be required (see Chapter 2 of this monograph).

CONCLUSION

The data from this study show high congruence among what individuals want from a self-help group, what they report actually occurs in these groups, how satisfied they are, and what they like best about the self-help group. There was also a high degree of consistency between the reports of the treatment and case study samples. Respondents reported that they want social support, both emotional and informational, from their self-help group, and this is mainly what they receive. The fact that almost one-third of the treatment sample belongs to more than one self-help group indicates both the high need of these families and the high degree of satisfaction they obtain from group participation.

It is important to recognize that the membership of self-help groups consists of self-selected individuals. As can be seen from the study sample descriptions, membership of self-help groups for the mentally ill represents primarily a middle class population, although a sizable minority in our sample were working-class members. Other studies of self-help groups (9, 16) also find them to be composed principally of middle class individuals. Thus one unanswered question is, "Are the needs of working-class families of the mentally ill being adequately addressed?" In the Pittsburgh study, eight new self-help groups for families of the mentally ill were organized. The groups had little difficulty in recruiting and keeping members, except for one group that was located in a predominately working-class community. To organize self-help groups in urban, working-class communities, planners may need to operate through the natural, neighborhood-based systems of informal support in these communities (23, 24). Such an organizational strategy is quite different from intervention through community mental health centers, which is successful in communities that are predominately middle class. Further research and the development of model interventions are needed to explore this issue.

Clearly, neither self-help groups nor any one intervention modality can meet all the needs of families of the mentally ill. As the data show, self-help group activities are only infrequently focused on behavioral change and structured or directive activities. For some families, the social support they receive through the self-help group may be insufficient; they may also require professional interventions designed to promote behavioral change and improve interaction between the mentally ill member of the family and other family members. A key unanswered question is whether membership in a self-help group together with additional professional intervention is more effective for families than either one or the other by itself. It must be recognized, of course, that professional interventions vary widely and may include modalities such as individual counseling, family therapy, group therapy, or the formation of psychoeducational groups. Research relating each of these varied interventions with membership in self-help groups is needed. In addition, we need to know whether professional and self-help interventions are best provided simultaneously or in sequence.

There are a number of other unanswered questions about self-help groups for families of the mentally ill that future research needs to address. First, to what extent is the local, community-based nature of self-help groups for families of the mentally ill related to their effectiveness? In other words, are these groups more effective because their membership tends to be homogeneous rather than heterogeneous in nature?

Second, why are some self-help group members helped more than other members? What variables are the most critical in this relationship? The data from this study suggest that patient functioning is one such important variable. Further investigation of this issue is needed. The answers to this question are very important in helping professionals design and tailor interventions to meet the specific needs of families of the mentally ill. Third, we need to find out the impact of factors such as group composition, group leadership, and group activities on the functioning of self-help groups.

Finally, research is needed on how members change as a result of self-help group participation. Strongly designed, longitudinal studies are needed to address this issue. Such research needs to take two important issues into account. As our data show, many families of the mentally ill join a self-help group anywhere from two to 10 years after diagnosis of their mentally ill relative. Thus researchers studying these families will begin their data collection at T1 well after the beginnings of stress are felt by families. As self-help groups for families of the mentally ill continue to expand, however, it may be possible to obtain data from families of newly diagnosed patients. This would allow comparison of the effects of self-help group membership on families of newly and previously diagnosed patients. Another complicating factor is that members of self-help groups for the mentally ill may be affected as much by change in patient behavior and functioning, which the self-help group can only minimally affect, as by the self-help group participation itself. Patient as well as family data over several time points must be collected to establish the independent and/or interdependent effects of these variables.

References

1. Biegel D, Shore BK, Gordon E: Building Support Networks for the Elderly: Theory and Applications. Beverly Hills, Sage Publications, 1984

2. Frankfather DL, Smith MJ, Caro FG: Family Care of the Elderly: Public Initiatives and Private Obligations. Lexington, MA, Lexington Books, 1981

3. Friedrich WN, Friedrich WL: Psychosocial assets of handicapped and non-handicapped children. Am J Ment Defic 85:551–553, 1981

4. Johnson FL, Rudolf LA, Hartman JR: Helping the family cope with childhood cancer. Psychosomatics 20:241–251, 1979

5. Creer C, Wing JK: Schizophrenia at Home. England, National Schizophrenia Fellowship, 1974

6. Doll W: Family coping with the mentally ill: an unanticipated problem of deinstitutionalization. Hosp Community Psychiatry 27:183–185, 1976

7. Falloon IRH, Boyd JL, McGill CW: Family Care of Schizophrenia: A Problem-Solving Approach to the Treatment of Mental Illness. New York, Guilford Press, 1984

8. Hatfield AB: Mental Illness—Impact on the Family. Paper presented at the 54th Annual Meeting of the American Orthopsychiatric Association, New York, April 1977

9. Hatfield AB: Psychological costs of schizophrenia to the family. Social Work 355–359, 1978

10. Lamb HR: Treating the Long Term Mentally Ill—Beyond Deinstitutionalization. San Francisco, Jossey-Bass, 1982

11. Lamb HR, Oliphant E: Schizophrenia through the eyes of families. Hosp Community Psychiatry 29:803–806, 1978

12. Leff JP: The management of the family of the chronic psychiatric patient, in The Chronic Psychiatric Patient in the Community: Principles of Treatment. Edited by Barofsky I, Budson RD. New York, SP Medical & Scientific Books, 1983

13. Hatfield AB: Self-help groups for families of the mentally ill. Social Work 26:408–413, 1981

14. Hatfield AB: Help-seeking behavior in families of schizophrenics. Am J Community Psychol 7:563–569, 1979

15. Levy L: The National Schizophrenia Fellowship—A British self-help group. Soc Psychiatry 16:129–135, 1981

16. Holden DF, Lewine RJ: How families evaluate mental health professionals, resources and effects of illness. Schizophr Bull 8:626–633, 1982

17. Mark MM, Cook TD: Design of randomized experiments and quasi-experiments, in Evaluation Research Methods: A Basic Guide. Edited by Rutman L. Beverly Hills, Sage Publications, 1984

18. Pasaminick B: Schizophrenics in the Community—An Experimental Study in the Prevention of Hospitalization. New York, Appleton-Century-Crofts, 1967

19. Levy L: Processes and activities in groups, in Self-Help Groups for Coping With Crisis. Edited by Lieberman MA, Borman LD. San Francisco, Jossey-Bass, 1979

20. Shulman L: Identifying, Measuring and Teaching Helping Skills. New York, Council on Social Work Education, 1981

21. Carkhuff RR: The Art of Helping. Amherst, MA, Human Resource Development Press, 1975

22. Carkhuff RR, Berenson BG: Beyond Counseling and Therapy. New York, Holt, Rinehart & Winston, 1967

23. Biegel D: Help-seeking and receiving in urban ethnic neighborhoods—strategies for empowerment. Journal of Prevention and Human Services 3:119–143, 1984

24. Naparstek A, Biegel D, Spiro H: Neighborhood Networks for Humane Mental Health Care. New York, Plenum Press, 1982

5

Heterogeneous Needs of Families of Schizophrenic Patients: Gender Differences

Mary V. Seeman, M.D.

5

Heterogeneous Needs of Families of Schizophrenic Patients: Gender Differences

Immediate families of victims of schizophrenia have much in common. They are called upon to understand and adapt to a recurring pattern of psychotic crisis, repeated periods of convalescence that are dysfunctional and lengthy, failed expectations, disrupted intimacy, inadequate delivery of helpful services, imperfect responses to imperfect therapies, and, worst of all, the perceived blame of others such as relatives, friends, neighbors, and those who should know better, the mental health professionals (1–4). What these families also have in common is their innocence. They are blameless for the schizophrenia in their family but are nevertheless ashamed (5). They are also rudderless, lost in a profusion of conflicting theories and paralyzed by the contradictory advice they often receive. Ashamed and rudderless, they are kept ignorant by well-meaning professional tenets of confidentiality and by professionals' impassioned conviction that diagnostic labeling hinders recovery (6). They are also imperiled sometimes by the impulsivity, destruc-

The author wishes to acknowledge Donna Gray for her invaluable contribution to the schizophrenia program at the Clarke Institute of Psychiatry, and Bill Jefferies, Founder of the Canadian Friends of Schizophrenics and President of the World Schizophrenia Fellowship, for continuing inspiration.

tivity, and unpredictability of their ill relative's behavior (1). This monograph has focused on the many ways in which sympathetic, well-timed interventions can address the many needs that families of schizophrenics share.

There is much, however, that is not common to all families of schizophrenics. Like all families, they come from different ethnocultural backgrounds and different socioeconomic levels. They profess varying levels of general education and varying levels of psychological sophistication. They have different perspectives on mental illness, different belief systems, different personal histories, unique personalities and coping styles, and variable family constellations, and they are distinguished by a wide range of available social supports (2).

They also have in their midst different patient relatives to whom they must adapt. Although all are ill with schizophrenia, they differ in the form of the syndrome from which they suffer, in the behaviors they exhibit, in the severity and duration of their symptoms, in their relative dangerousness and acknowledgment of illness, in their degree of dependence or self-reliance, in their phase of illness, in their response to treatment, and in the quality of their relationship with the nuclear family.

For these reasons, options for interventions need to be flexible and varied. Group approaches, moreover, need to be supplemented by individual interventions with families in need (7).

To illustrate only one significant variation in families of schizophrenics, the needs of families with ill daughters are to be compared in this chapter with the usually more serious needs (8) of families with ill sons. The burden on the families with schizophrenic daughters is perceived as lighter (9). Perhaps for this reason, family support organizations for schizophrenia consist mainly of families with ill sons (10).

WHY ARE DAUGHTERS LESS BURDENSOME?

Because they are women, schizophrenic daughters tend to be less aggressive (11), less likely to commit suicide (12), less likely to be involved with the law, less threatening to others, and more likely to acknowledge the authority of the parent or the doctor and adhere to a treatment regime (13).

Because the onset age for schizophrenia is later in women than it is in men (14), women are more likely to have completed their education, to be better versed in social skills, to have more friends, and to have some experience with employment. Women are more likely than men to have experienced intimacy, perhaps accompanied by marriage and motherhood. In other words, women have more to return to after an episode of illness (15).

Because of rearing differences between men and women, women are better able to cook, mend, launder, iron, clean house, wash dishes, shop, budget, and groom themselves. Thus even when unemployed outside the home, they are helpful within it. Men, in contrast, are reared for positions outside the home. When they fail to achieve the positions in life for which they were raised, their frustration and disappointment is greater, and their presence in the home is seen as a hindrance and an extra demand on the parents, usually the mother (16).

Because women do not usually fall ill until they have left the parental home, parents are less likely to blame themselves for their daughters' illness. They can project the blame onto others more effectively than they are able to do when this happens to sons, who are often still in high school and still relatively unexposed to outside social influences (16).

Frequency of acute episodes is lower in women, duration of hospitalization is shorter, and quality of remission is superior (17). All this lightens the burden for families.

Maintenance drug doses are lower in women (18) so that certain side effects are less severe (19). Tardive dyskinesia is thought to be more prevalent in women, but the heightened incidence is postmenopausal and not of immediate concern to the families of young schizophrenics. The more frightening (to the sufferer and to the family) unwanted effects (oculo-gyric crises, and acute dystonias) are more frequent in men (19).

WHAT ARE THE CONCERNS OF THE FAMILIES OF SCHIZOPHRENIC WOMEN?

Families of ill daughters worry about how the illness and its treatment will affect the attractiveness of their daughters and the likelihood of their attracting suitable mates. They worry about the weight gain, self-neglect, and skin eruptions that are a product of both the illness and the drug treatment. They worry about illness and drug-induced passivity, how it permits their daughters to become victims of violence, theft, and sexual abuse. They worry about the possibility of pregnancies and the care of children their daughters may bear. They worry about the substandard housing, the downtown districts their daughters migrate to. They worry about social programs for ex-patients that require nighttime travel on public transportation (20).

WHAT ARE THE CONCERNS OF THE FAMILIES OF SCHIZOPHRENIC MEN?

Of utmost concern for families of schizophrenic men are the possibility of suicide, possibility of aggression inside and outside the family home, sometimes unacceptable sexual impulses, lack of job or education, lack of interest in friendships or activities, continuing dependence on the family for everyday survival, unhygienic surroundings they live in, lack of attention to general health and grooming, denial of illness, failure to adhere to a treatment program, failure to express positive affect, abuse of alcohol and other drugs, poor diet, and preoccupation with potentially explosive ideas (20).

The intervention programs targeted to reduce high expressed emotion (EE) (21) are based on data correlating high EE in a family member with frequent relapse in the one- to two-year period following discharge. But these correlations apply only to the males in the cumulative sample of study subjects (22). Males may be more at risk because of greater face-to-face contact with a high EE family member, fewer social skills, more exposure to street drugs, lesser likelihood of a marital relationship, and more parental conflict (22). They may also be less likely to be taking appropriate (that is, not too high and not too low) doses of neuroleptic medication, or they may be more sensitive, for unknown reasons, to criticism and involvement by high EE family members. Since the mother is most often the high EE relative, mother–son relationships may be experientially and symbolically distinct in many ways from mother–daughter dyads.

RECOMMENDATIONS

Families of men with schizophrenia probably require specific interventions aimed at reducing parental expectations, acknowledging and dispelling self-blame, and suggesting problem-solving options for their sons that involve the visuospatial mode that men are particularly good at, rather than options that require language (23). These families need special support in coping with anger, aggressiveness, and the threat of suicide.

Families need help in addressing the difficulty of illness denial and treatment resistance. They need education about drug effects and withdrawal effects, since men stop and start medication. They need specific help with the defect symptoms to which men are more prone (24). They also need help in EE reduction and the reduction of face-to-face contact.

Families of women schizophrenics need something different: encouragement to help their daughters be more assertive and less victimized. They need help in deemphasizing physical attractiveness and promoting nurturant qualities so that their daughters, as employees, aunts, baby-sitters, and mothers, can deploy their often well-preserved affect in the service of those whose lives they influence. Reduction of EE in these families may be less productive than the sharing of experience (25) and the promotion of support networks (2).

Since families of schizophrenics differ in many significant

ways, not just in the gender of their ill relative, tailor-made intervention programs need to be developed to address their specific needs.

References

1. Lamb HR, Oliphant E: Schizophrenia through the eyes of families. Hosp Community Psychiatry 29:803–806, 1978

2. Potasznik H, Nelson G: Stress and social support: the burden experienced by the family of a mentally ill person. Am J Community Psychol 12:589–607, 1984

3. Terkelsen K: Schizophrenia and the family, II: adverse effects of family therapy. Fam Process 22:191–200, 1983

4. Thornton J, Plummer E, Seeman MV, et al: The family's reaction to schizophrenic illness. International Journal of Family Psychiatry 3:33–44, 1982

5. Hatfield AB: Psychological costs of schizophrenia to the family. Social Work 23:355–359, 1978

6. Hoffman B: To tell or not to tell. Schizophr Bull 7:369–371, 1981

7. Levene J, Jeffries JJ, Newman F: Focal family therapy: a component in the treatment of schizophrenia. International Journal of Family Psychiatry 5:3–19, 1985

8. Seeman MV, Hauser P: Schizophrenia: the influence of gender on family environment. International Journal of Family Psychiatry 5:227–232, 1984

9. Gibbons JS, Horn SH, Powell JM, et al: Schizophrenic patients and their families: a survey in a psychiatric service based on a DGH unit. Br J Psychiatry 144:70–77, 1984

10. Seeman MV: Report on a survey of Canadian Friends of Schizophrenics. Am J Psychiatry 140:1648, 1983

11. Watt NF: Patterns of childhood and social development in adult schizophrenia. Arch Gen Psychiatry 35:160–165, 1978

12. Roy A: Suicide in chronic schizophrenia. Br J Psychiatry 141:171–177, 1982

13. Keskiner A, Zelman J, Ruppert EH: Advantages of being female in psychiatric rehabilitation. Arch Gen Psychiatry 28:689–692, 1973

14. Loranger AW: Sex differences in age at onset of schizophrenia. Arch Gen Psychiatry 41:157–161, 1984

15. Seeman MV: Gender differences in schizophrenia. Can J Psychiatry 27:107–112, 1982

16. Seeman MV: Schizophrenic men and women require different treatment programs. Journal of Psychiatric Treatment and Evaluation 5:143–148, 1983

17. Salokangas RKR: Prognostic implications of the sex of schizophrenic patients. Br J Psychiatry 142:145–151, 1983

18. Seeman MV: Interaction of sex, age, and neuroleptic dose. Compr Psychiatry 24:125–128, 1983

19. Ayd FJ Jr: Survey of drug-induced extrapyramidal reactions. JAMA 175:1054–1061, 1961

20. Hauser P, Pollock B, Finkelberg F, et al: Risk and protective factors in schizophrenia: clinical and social implications. Modern Medicine 40:579–584, 1985

21. Barrowclough C, Tarrier N: 'Psychosocial' interventions with families and their effects on the course of schizophrenia: a review. Psychol Med 14:629–642, 1984

22. Vaughn CE, Snyder KS, Jones S, et al: Family factors in schizophrenic relapse. Arch Gen Psychiatry 41:1169–1177, 1984

23. McGlone J: Sex differences in human brain asymmetry: a critical survey. Behav Brain Sciences 3:215–263, 1980

24. Lewine RRJ, Burbach D, Meltzer HY: Effect of diagnostic criteria on the ratio of male to female schizophrenic patients. Am J Psychiatry 141:84–87, 1984

25. Thornton JF, Plummer E, Seeman MV, et al: Schizophrenia: group support for relatives. Can J Psychiatry 26:341–344, 1981

6

Medical Students' Attitudes Toward Psychiatry, Schizophrenic Patients, and Their Families

Leah J. Dickstein, M.D.
Marion Zucker Goldstein, M.D.
Judith J. Stephenson, S.M.
Horatio Fabrega, Jr., M.D.
Nadine Robles, Ph.D.

6

Medical Students' Attitudes Toward Psychiatry, Schizophrenic Patients, and Their Families

Medical educators continue to debate the accuracy and effects of the 1980 congressionally sponsored Graduate Medical Education National Advisory Committee (GMENAC) report (1) on future needs and opportunities for physicians, especially in light of its forecast of a shortage of psychiatrists and the fact that many students choose family practice. Medical educators also continue to evaluate and alter current medical school curricula to ensure that students are taught to be humanistic physicians, as outlined in the 1984 Panel on the General Professional Education of the Physician (GPEP) report (2). Generally, psychiatric educators assume much of the responsibility for teaching and training all medical students to relate and respond sensitively and knowledgeably to all patients.

Knowledge of medical students' attitudes toward not only psychiatry in general but also specific issues in psychiatry such as the treatment of schizophrenic patients and their families will enable educators to influence these attitudes more directly and more rationally.

We chose to survey attitudes toward schizophrenic patients because they typify the difficult-to-treat chronic mental patients who, at various stages of illness, may become the responsibility of many nonpsychiatric physicians for comprehensive care.

Our objectives for this study were to discover

1. Students' attitudes toward psychiatry
2. How students feel about working with schizophrenic patients
3. How medical students perceive their roles as practicing physicians in communicating with patients' families
4. How a physician's personal, family, and social background influences his or her approach to patients

We surveyed junior medical students at two large institutions: the University of Pittsburgh, Pennsylvania, and the University of Louisville, Kentucky. Our procedures and findings are discussed in this chapter.

Surveys of Medical Students' Attitudes: 1960–1984

More than two decades ago, Hill (3) wrote that medical students' attitudes toward psychiatry are formed long before their clerkships. These attitudes stem from opinions they begin forming in childhood and adolescence, as undergraduates, and from varied influences and experiences in medical school.

Elizur and Rosenheim (4) observed that medical students' empathy for the mentally ill can be temporarily increased when the students participate in a self-exploratory group during their psychiatric clerkship. Maxmen (5) discovered that students developed more favorable attitudes toward psychiatry, psychiatrists, and the treatability of psychiatric patients through the clerkship. Burra et al. (6) discerned positive, though only temporary, changes in students' attitudes toward psychiatry after the clerkship. Kaplan-DeNour and Weisstub (7) found senior medical students to be slightly more negative than junior students in their attitude toward people with emotional problems. They mentioned that the psychiatric clerkship had not changed this outlook and, in fact, seemed to have increased dissatisfaction with psychiatry.

Antonovsky's program (8) emphasized that "real medicine" always includes the spectrum of emotional health to emotional illness. From the first year on emphasis is on a holistic view of patients both theoretically and experientially.

At the University of British Columbia, Maurice et al. (9) designed the clerkship so that students served as primary therapists. Important positive outcomes where found in students' attitudes toward mental illness and the rotation in general. Meltzer and Grigorian (10) noted that changes in students' attitudes toward mental illness depended on interest in psychiatry as a career choice and on "style of intellectual ability." Students who modified their opinions and became empathic and less authoritarian in their views evidenced more psychiatric career interest.

A survey of Swedish students by Arn et al. (11) revealed that the experience of the psychiatry course itself was just one factor making for more positive attitudes toward mental disorder and psychiatric care. Other factors contributing to the possession of more positive attitudes were being female, being politically radical, and having a family history of mental disorder.

Orleans et al. (12) learned that good rapport with supervisors and patients was strongly related to positive attitudes toward psychiatry; Nielsen and Eaton (13) noticed that students liked working directly with patients and also liked to observe psychiatrists doing so.

Bashook and Weissman's (14) survey of students' perceptions of the psychiatric clerkship disclosed that students consider it "easy," whereas Yager et al. (15) concluded from their survey that students view psychiatry as worthwhile although imprecise and lacking in prestige. The students also felt that nonphysicians could manage most psychiatric patients.

Ghadirian et al. (16) compared two surveys completed by third-year students 10 years apart. In the second survey, students remarked that they found clinical aspects of training, especially psychotherapy, more important than the theoretical and research material presented.

Lau and Oxford (17), in studying student attitudes toward psychiatric clerkships, emphasized what may usually be overlooked, that is, the importance of identifying students who may be personally vulnerable to the stresses of the clerkship. Johnson et al. (18) also discovered that psychiatry evoked unpleasant personal feelings in some students. Light's (19) study of students' attitudes points out a current dilemma: Although students ascribe characteristics of a good clinician to psychiatrists, they believe psychiatrists lack the technological medical skills of general physicians.

Finally, Yager et al. (20) found that, whereas students choosing a career in psychiatry were more likely to want personal counseling and were less likely to refer a relative for counseling, those not selecting a psychiatric career wanted more group seminars on stress and on personal, academic, and career concerns and were more likely to refer a relative for counseling. A review of the cited surveys is presented in Table 1.

CHARACTERISTICS OF THE TWO SCHOOLS SURVEYED

Each University of Pittsburgh class consists of approximately 140 students, 30 percent women and 70 percent men. Each student has a personal faculty adviser as well as an upper-class student adviser. Three years ago, 700 requests to volunteer to become student advisers were sent to faculty. After 100 faculty had volunteered by mail, an additional 50 were recruited to have one adviser for each medical student. With two students calling advisers during the first week of school and inviting them to meet their advisees, the program has been 40 percent effective this year (Lois Pounds, M.D., Associate Dean of Student Affairs; personal communication, October 1985).

There are several resources for students with nonacademic problems, including the University Counseling Center, which is staffed by psychologists. For the past six years, a clinical psychiatric social worker has been available exclusively for

Table 1. Review of Surveys Cited

Date	Author	School	Number of Students Surveyed	Attitudes/Results Found
1977	Antonovsky	Ben Gurion University of the Neger Bersheba, Israel	*	Improvement in attitude toward persons with emotional problems as part of general medicine.
1971	Arn	Limea, Sweden*	59	More positive attitude after basic psychiatry course toward mental disorders and mental care.
1982	Bashook	15 American medical schools	680	Perceptions of psychiatric clerkship's being easy.
1982	Burra	Queens University Kingston, Ontario Canada	189	Positive change in attitude among medical students toward psychiatry was transient.
1981	DeNour	Hebrew University Hadassah Medical School Israel	1st yr. 76 5th yr. 38	Psychiatric clerkship did not change attitudes toward people with emotional problems, possibly increased dissatisfaction with psychiatry.
1982	Elizur	Sackler School of Medicine Tel Aviv University Tel Aviv Bar Ilan University Ramat Gan, Israel	153 299	Attitude toward psychiatry changed temporarily with participation in a self-exploratory group during the clerkship.

1982	Ghadirian	McGill University Montreal, Quebec Canada	227	Attitudes toward psychiatry were found to be specific to certain areas. They were positive about clinical training, psychotherapy and organic therapy and negative toward research and theory.
1960	Hill	*	*	Changed in positive direction toward mental illness after clerkship and self-exploratory group experience.
1977	Johnson	University of Southern California Los Angeles, Cal.	196	Found certain topics in psychiatry curriculum are needed by all physicians, not just psychiatrists.
1976	Lau	University of Ottawa Ottawa, Canada	67	Attitudes toward psychiatry improved after clerkship, especially toward psychiatry.
1975	Light	Tufts University Boston, Mass.	*	Attitudes toward psychiatry, psychiatrists and good clinicians are conflicted.
1975	Maurice	University of British Columbia, Vancouver, British Columbia, Canada	31	Attitudes toward psychiatric illness were modestly changed in positive manner.
1979	Maxmen	Albert Einstein College of Medicine Bronx Municipal Hospital Bronx, N.Y.	111	After clerkship, developed more favorable attitudes toward psychiatry, psychiatrists, and patients.
1972	Meltzer	George Washington University Washington, D.C.	83	Positive attitude change toward mental illness.

Table 1. Review of Surveys Cited

Date	Author	School	Number of Students Surveyed	Attitudes/Results Found
1981	Nielsen	Georgetown University George Washington University Washington, D.C.	204	Most were favorable to psychiatry and psychiatrists.
1980	Orleans	Duke University North Carolina	92	Positive relationships among supervisors, students, and patients were strongly related to favorable attitudes.
1983	Wilkinson	King's College Hospital, London, England	94	Attitudes toward psychiatry, psychiatric patients and a career in psychiatry.
1983	Wilkinson	King's College Hospital, London, England	94	Attitudes to psychiatry maintained one year later with one changing significantly, i.e., fewer agreed psychiatrists are held in poor regard by most other physicians.
1982	Yager	UCLA Los Angeles, Cal.	344	Attitudes toward psychiatry related to psychiatry as a career choice, desire for mental health services and experiences in psychiatry courses.
1982	Yager	UCLA Los Angeles, Cal.	572	Attitudes toward psychiatry similar: worthwhile but low prestige.

* Information not available in article

medical students one day per week to evaluate and offer or refer for psychotherapy. This social worker also holds stress management workshops after orientation day at the start of medical school. The Diagnostic Evaluation Center of the psychiatry department is available as well. The director of the medical student psychiatry curriculum, Dr. Horatio Fabrega, is sensitive to providing and encourages students to seek appropriate psychiatric contacts, and the assistant dean, associate dean, and dean of student affairs are also available and concerned with personal and nonacademic student well-being. The only event to which medical students' families are invited is a preorientation picnic. The alumni association provides a cocktail party for incoming students only.

Regarding curriculum, the second year students have six weeks of clinical skills, which coordinates with their learning to do physical examinations and histories. During this year they receive their first formal introduction to Clinical Psychiatry in the form of lectures, clinical demonstrations, and small group teaching experiences. In the third year, the students have a six-week clerkship in psychiatry during which they are assigned to one of five specialty modules: schizophrenia, adolescent, geriatric, affective disorders, and consultation–liaison. During this clerkship, medical students listen to nursing reports each morning and go on rounds with faculty, psychiatric resident social worker, and primary nurse. They are assigned to approximately six patients and participate in team decisions. They present at team meetings and attend weekly case conferences on the specialty modules and didactic sessions made available by faculty. Part of each week is spent on other units, visiting an alcohol rehabilitation center, a state hospital, and a children's service. The curriculum director conducts daily case conferences that all the students attend and in which a variety of individual patients including schizophrenic patients are presented. The medical students also rotate through the Diagnostic Evaluation Center, the equivalent of a psychiatric emergency room. Electives in psychiatry are available for students in their fourth year.

Each University of Louisville class consists of 124 students, approximately 40 percent women and 60 percent men. Each student is assigned a sophomore buddy before school starts and is invited to participate in a Health Awareness Workshop with their significant others the week before medical school classes start. Workshop participants are divided into large didactic and small interactional groups for four half-days of meetings as well as for evening activities. Topics covered include the responsiblity for self-awareness and health care, the psychobiology of illness, wellness and stress, stress reduction, the importance of nutrition and exercise, relaxation techniques, constructive coping in relationships, medical ethics, religious faith and health, the history of the medical school, an introduction to Louisville, a tour of the Health Sciences Center, nutritional lunches, health checks, athletic events, picnics, an evening devoted to physicians and the arts, time management, study skills and test taking, a support session specifically for significant others, and a special program for children. Those who attend are divided into groups by unit labs with their own year-long sophomore and faculty health tutors (advisers) who continue the small group support sessions and are available individually throughout the year. The message to all is simple and clear—meet, know, and care for yourselves, each other, and your significant others, and we are all here to help you at any time with any problem that affects you. In addition, there is a special orientation program for minority students.

There are several gratis university resources for personal and confidential counseling. The associate dean of student affairs, as the psychiatric consultant to the University Counseling Center and psychiatrist to the Health Sciences Center students, is available half-time, with a postgraduate year (PGY) 4 psychiatry resident on this rotation for six months who is available three half-days per week. The counseling center staff of clinical and educational psychologists and graduate trainees are also available, and both psychiatric faculty and clinical faculty see students occasionally. The dean of student affairs is also available to assist students with referrals for their families if couple therapy is not indicated. Intermittent support and information programs are held during the academic year for preclinical students to discuss any problems and concerns related to school, the season (the long winter days or difficult holidays), or forthcoming clinical rotations and concomitant anxieties. It has been our experience that women students, in particular, need reassurance about spending so much time away from their families. Special programs are held that deal with impairment secondary to alcohol and drug abuse, and significant others are invited. In addition, by invitation from the Medical Student Spouses Auxiliary, the psychiatric consultant discusses common stresses, concerns, and possible constructive coping mechanisms for married students.

The psychiatry curriculum consists of electives for the preclinical years and the sophomore behavioral sciences 56-hour core lecture course, which includes additional individual experiences in patient interviewing. In the third year, the six-week clerkship consists of a core lecture series and a choice of rotations at a child guidance clinic, a university acute-care inpatient unit and an outpatient unit, an emergency psychiatry service, a consultation–liaison service, a Veterans Administration hospital acute-care inpatient unit, and two inpatient units (an adolescent and an adult service) in a private university-affiliated hospital. All of these units are general units in which patients with a variety of psychiatric disorders are treated. In addition, night-call assignments at the University Emergency Psychiatry Service provide numerous opportunities for students to observe and interact with schizophrenic patients and their families in crisis. Visits are scheduled to a state hospital, a drug and alcohol treatment center, and a partial hospitalization program. At each clerkship site, students attend daily staff meetings, weekly case conferences, and journal clubs. They work with patients under close supervision, attend all family conferences, and write a clinical psychotherapy paper. In addition, the department chairman holds clinical rounds at each location once during each rotation. A variety of psychiatry electives are available to senior students. In addition, faculty are interested in helping students develop feasible individual elective courses.

METHOD

We carried out our study of junior medical students' attitudes at the University of Louisville and the University of Pittsburgh as the students entered and exited from their psychiatry clerkships. In addition to obtaining demographic data, we administered two questionnaires (see Appendix). The first was Wilkinson et al.'s (21) 1980 questionnaire, which was developed to elicit attitudes toward psychiatry from medical students before and after they took an eight-week psychiatry clerkship at King's College Hospital, London, England and one year after this clerkship.

This 18-item attitude questionnaire was used in the present study to assess students' attitudes toward psychiatry both before the psychiatry clerkship began and after the clerkship had been completed. The individual items concern attitudes toward psychiatrists, psychiatry, psychiatric patients, and psychiatric treatment. According to Wilkinson et al. (22), nine of the 18 items (2, 5–7, 11, 13–15, 17) express positive views, and the remaining nine (1, 3, 4, 8–10, 12, 16, 18) express negative views. Items are measured on a 4-point scale ranging from "strongly disagree" (1) to "strongly agree" (4). In addition, students were asked to indicate their intention to specialize in psychiatry on a 4-point scale ranging from "no, definitely" (1) to "yes, definitely" (4).

The second questionnaire, the Medical Student Questionnaire, was developed for this study by our authors Goldstein, Fabrega, and Robles to assess medical students' attitudes toward schizophrenic patients and their families. The questionnaire contains an introduction that states that mental health professionals other than physicians have been inclined to assume the care-giving role toward patients' families. In the questionnaire, the students are asked to state what they want to learn pertaining to families of schizophrenic patients. They are also asked to explain how they perceive their roles as practicing physicians in regard to these families. The last question asks how aspects of their personal backgrounds are related to their approach to patients and patients' families.

We ran trial assessments during 1984 and collected the questionnaire data for our 1985 study from 127 junior students before and after their psychiatry rotations. At the University of Louisville, the questionnaires were given on a voluntary basis to 63 students in three consecutive rotations: 54 pairs of before-clerkship and after-clerkship questionnaires were returned, with a response rate of 86 percent. Of these 54 pairs, 33 were completed, and 21 pairs lacked the after-clerkship attitude toward psychiatry questionnaire. At the University of Pittsburgh, 81 questionnaries were given on a voluntary basis during five rotations: 73 pairs of before- and after-clerkship questionnaires were returned, for a response rate of 90 percent.

DATA ANALYSIS

An analysis of variance was used to determine pre- and postclerkship differences in attitudes and to elicit differences between students at the two schools in their attitudes toward schizophrenia, schizophrenic patients, and the families of schizophrenic patients.

Chi-square values were obtained for the item-by-item evaluation to see if there was a shift in response from pre- to postclerkship.

The Sign test was applied to pre- and post-clerkship positive and negative changes toward psychiatry for each school and for the sample as a whole.

RESULTS

Sample Characteristics

Demographic. Table 2 presents the demographic characteristics of the samples from the two schools. The two samples

Table 2. Demographics of Students

Characteristic	Louisville	Pittsburgh	Total
Number of participating students	54	73	127
Mean age in years	25.4	25.5	25.5
Gender			
Males (n = 90)	76%	67%	71%
Females (n = 37)	24%	33%	29%
Marital Status			
Married (n = 25)	22%	18%	20%
Single (n = 98)	74%	79%	77%
Divorced or Separated (n = 4)	4%	3%	3%

differed little in terms of mean age, gender, and marital status. At both schools, approximately 10 percent of the nonmarried students were living with a significant other, and 30 percent of the married students had at least one child.

Descriptive. As can be seen in Table 3, half of the students' undergraduate majors were biology, approximately 20 percent were chemistry, and the remainder were in other areas. This breakdown reflects the age-old constrictive education rather than the broad-based education in the humanities that the GPEP report supports.

Half of the Louisville students and 37 percent of the Pittsburgh students knew someone with a psychiatric disorder. Seventeen percent from Louisville and 22 percent from Pittsburgh knew a therapist, and 19 percent from Louisville and 16 percent from Pittsburgh had worked in a mental health facility. Specialty choices matched the national average and were similar for both schools. Two percent of the Louisville students and eight percent of the Pittsburgh students identified psychiatry as their specialty choice both before and after the clerkship. Because of the small number who identified psychiatry as their specialty choice (n = 6), no connection can be made between those who knew a therapist and/or worked in a mental health facility and those who chose psychiatry as their specialty. From

Table 3. Descriptive Characteristics of Students

Characteristic	Percentage of Louisville Students	Percentage of Pittsburgh Students	Total Percentage
Undergraduate major			
Biology (n = 58)	52	42	46
Chemistry (n = 27)	20	22	21
Psychology (n = 5)	2	6	4
Other (n = 37)	26	30	29
Number of undergraduate psychology courses			
None (n = 23)	22	15	18
1 Course (n = 39)	33	29	31
2–3 Courses (n = 47)	37	38	37
4+ Courses (n = 17)	8	18	14
Prior relationship with person who had a psychiatric disorder			
Yes (n = 54)	52	37	43
No (n = 71)	48	63	57
Are any family members or friends therapists or members of the psychiatric profession?			
Yes (n = 25)	17	22	20
No (n = 101)	83	78	80
Ever work in a psychiatric hospital or mental health unit?			
Yes (n = 21)	19	16	17
No (n = 104)	81	84	83
Identified specialty choice			
Psychiatry (n = 6)	2	8	5
Surgery (n = 33)	28	29	28
*Primary care (n = 59)	52	50	51
**Hospital-based (n = 18)	18	13	16
Uncertain about choice of speciality?			
Yes (n = 40)	28	34	32
No (n = 87)	72	66	68

*Primary care includes internal medicine, pediatrics, and family practice

**Hospital-based includes pathology, radiology, emergency medicine, and anesthesiology

the data, it appears that the junior psychiatry clerkship did not influence these students' choice in terms of psychiatry as a specialty.

Students' Attitudes Toward Psychiatry Before and After Clerkship

Eighteen student attitudes toward psychiatry before and after the psychiatric clerkship are shown for each school and for the total sample in Tables 4 and 5. The individual items were rated on a four-point scale, but the categories have been collapsed into two: agree ("strongly agree" "agree") and disagree ("strongly disagree" "disagree").

Using the Sign test, analysis of positive and negative attitudes revealed the following: Of the nine positive-attitude items on the Wilkinson et al. questionnaire, six showed no significant difference before and after clerkship. The item assessing the attitude that psychiatrists try to treat the whole patient and not just the disease (Item 5) showed an increase in agreement in the Louisville students, a decrease in agreement in the Pittsburgh students, and a decrease in agreement in the total sample. Items assessing beliefs that psychiatrists are at the forefront of the movement to humanize medicine and that the problems presented by psychiatric patients are often particularly interesting and challenging (Items 6 and 7, respectively) both showed statistically significant increases in agreement before and after clerkship.

Among the nine negative items, seven showed no significant difference before and after clerkship for the total sample. A significant decrease in agreement occurred for items assessing attitudes that psychiatrists tend to be more emotionally unstable than other doctors (Item 3) and that psychiatric patients hardly ever get better (Item 8).

Students' Attitudes Toward Schizophrenic Patients

Table 6 presents students' attitudes toward schizophrenic patients before the clerkship as represented by responses to the questionnaire developed for this study by our authors Goldstein, Fabrega, and Robles. Approximately 60 percent at both schools and in the total sample agreed that the assessment of a patient with a schizophrenic or other mental disorder is time consuming and emotionally draining. After the clerkship (see Table 7), about the same percentage of students felt the assessment was emotionally draining, but a lower percentage felt it was time consuming.

Students' Attitudes Toward Families of Schizophrenic Patients

Tables 8 and 9 present students' attitudes toward families of schizophrenic patients before and after the clerkship. No significant differences occurred between the two schools before and after the clerkship. Forty-two percent of the total sample agreed that families of schizophrenic patients are usually "emotionally disturbed." Although not to a statistically significant degree, more students had this perception at both schools after than before the clerkship. Most agreed that the physician's responsibility is not only toward the patient, and the total sample after the clerkship felt it is the physician's responsibility to address family issues of patients with schizophrenia as well. A slight increase occurred after the clerkship in the number of students who agreed that only the patient was the physician's responsibility and that families are the concern of social workers. The majority of students were aware of the value of a psychoeducational approach to families of schizophrenic patients before and after the clerkship and felt that it was their concern as physicians.

Students' Attitudes Toward Faculty Concern and Support

The majority of students in both schools agreed before and after the clerkship that faculty should be concerned about personal family and situations of the students (see Tables 10 and 11). The fact that in Pittsburgh more initiative is required of the student to obtain such concern than is required in Louis-

Table 4. Students' Attitudes Toward Psychiatry: Preclerkship

	Louisville				Pittsburgh				Total			
Questionnaire Item	*N*	Agree	*N*	Disagree	*N*	Agree	*N*	Disagree	*N*	Agree	*N*	Disagree
1. Psychiatric patients, generally speaking, are not easy to like	17	32%	37	68%	19	26%	53	74%	36	29%	90	71%
*2. Psychiatrists are, on the whole, less dogmatic than other doctors	27	51%	26	49%	30	42%	43	58%	57	46%	68	54%
3. Psychiatrists tend to be more emotionally unstable than other doctors	20	37%	34	63%	19	26%	53	74%	39	31%	87	69%**
4. Psychiatrists are held in poor regard by most other doctors	34	62%	20	38%	44	61%	28	39%	78	62%	48	38%
*5. Psychiatrists try to treat the whole patient and not just the disease	30	56%	24	44%	63	88%	9	12%	93	74%	33	26%**
*6. Psychiatrists are at the forefront of the movement to humanize medicine	29	55%	24	45%	34	48%	37	52%	63	51%	61	49%
*7. The problems presented by psychiatric patients are often particularly interesting and challenging	43	80%	11	20%	66	92%	6	8%	109	87%	17	13%
8. Psychiatric patients hardly ever get better	16	30%	38	70%	35	49%	37	51%	51	40%	75	60%
9. Psychiatric patients tend to make more emotional demands on their doctors than do other patients	39	72%	15	28%	60	83%	12	17%	99	79%	27	21%

10. Within medicine, psychiatry is one of the less important specialties	4	8%	50	92%	9	13%	63	87%	13	10%	113	90%
*11. Mental illness presents us with one of the great intellectual challenges in the field of medicine	46	85%	8	15%	64	89%	8	11%	110	87%	16	13%
12. Psychiatry is too inexact; it seems to lack a proper scientific basis	23	43%	31	57%	38	53%	34	47%	61	48%	65	52%
*13. Psychiatrists are more concerned than other doctors to establish rapport with their patients	37	69%	17	31%	52	75%	20	28%	89	71%	37	29%
*14. Too little time is devoted to psychiatry in the medical curriculum	17	32%	37	68%	34	48%	37	52%	51	41%	64	59%
*15. Psychiatric skills are essential in general practice	54	100%	0	0%	70	97%	2	3%	124	99%	2	1%
16. The practice of psychiatry is unrewarding because the treatment is so lengthy and the results so inconclusive	19	35%	35	65%	26	36%	46	64%	45	36%	81	64%
*17. Empathy with patients is as important as factual knowledge in clinical medicine	45	83%	9	17%	60	83%	12	17%	105	83%	21	17%
18. Psychiatrists are often failed physicians	2	4%	52	96%	1	1%	71	99%	3	2%	123	98%

*Positive items

**χ^2 = 14.678, 1 df, p = 0.0001

Table 5. Students' Attitudes Toward Psychiatry: Postclerkship

	Louisville				Pittsburgh				Total			
Questionnaire Item	*N*	Agree	*N*	Disagree	*N*	Agree	*N*	Disagree	*N*	Agree	*N*	Disagree
1. Psychiatric patients, generally speaking, are not easy to like	4	12%	29	88%	15	21%	58	79%	19	18%	87	82%
* 2. Psychiatrists are, on the whole, less dogmatic than other doctors	21	64%	12	36%	33	45%	40	55%	54	51%	52	49%
3. Psychiatrists tend to be more emotionally unstable than other doctors	5	15%	28	85%	15	21%	57	79%	20	19%	85	81%
4. Psychiatrists are held in poor regard by most other doctors	21	64%	12	36%	49	67%	24	33%	70	66%	36	34%
* 5. Psychiatrists try to treat the whole patient and not just the disease	20	61%	13	39%	50	69%	23	31%	70	66%	36	34%
* 6. Psychiatrists are at the forefront of the movement to humanize medicine	26	79%	7	21%	45	62%	28	38%	71	67%	35	33%
* 7. The problems presented by psychiatric patients are often particularly interesting and challenging	31	94%	2	6%	71	97%	2	3%	102	96%	4	4%
8. Psychiatric patients hardly ever get better	11	33%	22	67%	23	32%	49	68%	34	32%	71	68%
9. Psychiatric patients tend to make more emotional demands on their doctors than do other patients	29	88%	4	12%	58	80%	15	20%	87	82%	19	18%

10. Within medicine, psychiatry is one of the less important specialties	3	9%	30	91%	8	11%	65	89%	11	10%	95	90%
*11. Mental illness presents us with one of the great intellectual challenges in the field of medicine	29	88%	4	12%	63	88%	9	12%	92	88%	13	12%
12. Psychiatry is too inexact; it seems to lack a proper scientific basis	11	33%	22	67%	32	44%	40	56%	43	41%	62	59%
*13. Psychiatrists are more concerned than other doctors to establish rapport with their patients	22	67%	11	33%	55	76%	17	24%	77	73%	28	27%
*14. Too little time is devoted to psychiatry in the medical curriculum	16	49%	17	51%	28	39%	44	61%	44	42%	61	58%
*15. Psychiatric skills are essential in general practice	33	100%	0	0%	71	99%	1	1%	104	99%	1	1%
16. The practice of psychiatry is unrewarding because the treatment is so lengthy and the results so inconclusive	9	27%	24	73%	22	31%	50	69%	31	30%	74	70%
*17. Empathy with patients is as important as factual knowledge in clinical medicine	31	94%	2	6%	55	76%	17	24%	86	82%	19	18%**
18. Psychiatrists are often failed physicians	3	9%	30	91%	4	6%	68	94%	7	7%	98	93%

*positive items
**$\chi^2 = 3.593$, 1 df, $p = 0.058$

Table 6. Students' Attitudes Toward Schizophrenic Patients: Preclerkship

	Louisville				Pittsburgh				Total			
Questionnaire Item	*N*	Agree	*N*	Disagree	*N*	Agree	*N*	Disagree	*N*	Agree	*N*	Disagree
The assessment of a patient with a schizophrenic or other mental disorder is time-consuming	32	59%	22	41%	50	69%	23	31%	85	65%	45	35%
The assessment and treatment of a patient with schizophrenia is emotionally draining	34	63%	20	37%	53	74%	19	26%	87	69%	39	31%

Table 7. Students' Attitudes Toward Schizophrenic Patients: Postclerkship

	Louisville				Pittsburgh				Total			
Questionnaire Item	*N*	Agree	*N*	Disagree	*N*	Agree	*N*	Disagree	*N*	Agree	*N*	Disagree
The assessment of a patient with schizophrenia is time-consuming	19	35%	35	65%	39	53%	34	47%	58	46%	69	54%
The assessment of a patient with schizophrenia is emotionally draining	36	67%	18	33%	54	74%	19	26%	90	71%	37	29%

Table 8. Students' Attitudes Toward Families of Schizophrenic Patients: Preclerkship

Questionnaire Item	Louisville				Pittsburgh				Total			
	N	Agree	N	Disagree	N	Agree	N	Disagree	N	Agree	N	Disagree
Families of schizophrenic patients are usually emotionally disturbed	22	41%	32	59%	31	43%	41	57%	53	42%	73	58%
Physician's responsibility is toward patient only	3	6%	50	94%	5	7%	68	93%	8	6%	118	94%
It is the physician's responsibility to address family issues of patients with schizophrenia	52	96%	2	4%	72	99%	1	1%	124	98%	3	2%
Family issues are the concern of social workers only	0	0%	54	100%	0	0%	73	100%	0	0%	127	100%
As a future physician, developing a psychoeducational approach to families of schizophrenic patients is a concern of mine	39	75%	13	25%	60	83%	12	17%	99	80%	25	20%
I think a psychoeducational approach to families of schizophrenic patients can alleviate isolation and stress of family members	49	96%	2	4%	67	96%	3	4%	113	96%	5	4%

Table 9. Students' Attitudes Toward the Families of Schizophrenic Patients: Postclerkship

	Louisville				Pittsburgh				Total			
Questionnaire Item	*N*	Agree	*N*	Disagree	*N*	Agree	*N*	Disagree	*N*	Agree	*N*	Disagree
Families of schizophrenic patients are usually emotionally disturbed	27	50%	27	50%	40	55%	33	45%	67	53%	60	47%
Physician's responsibility is toward patient only	8	15%	46	85%	10	14%	63	86%	18	14%	109	86%
It is the physician's responsibility to address family issues of patients with schizophrenia	53	98%	1	2%	68	93%	5	7%	121	95%	6	5%
Family issues are the concern of social workers only	2	4%	52	96%	6	8%	67	92%	8	6%	118	94%
More emphasis on genetics, psychosocial community, and diagnostic chemotherapy issues would have made me more confident to develop a psychoeducational approach to families of schizophrenic patients	44	82%	10	18%	52	73%	19	27%	96	77%	29	23%
I think a psychoeducational approach to families of schizophrenic patients can alleviate isolation and stress of family members	52	96%	2	4%	72	99%	1	1%	124	98%	3	2%

Table 10. Students' Attitudes About Faculty Concern and Support: Preclerkship

	Louisville				Pittsburgh				Total			
	N	Agree	*N*	Disagree	*N*	Agree	*N*	Disagree	*N*	Agree	*N*	Disagree
Do you think medical school faculty *should* be concerned about personal family situations of their students?	45	85%	8	15%	51	70%	22	30%	96	76%	30	24%
I think that the medical faculty *actually* does show concern for my personal family situation.	25	50%	25	50%	16	22%	56	78%	41	34%	81	64%*

*$\chi^2 = 8.997$, 1 df, $p = 0.0027$

Table 11. Students' Attitudes About Faculty Concern and Support: Postclerkship

	Louisville				Pittsburgh				Total			
	N	Agree	*N*	Disagree	*N*	Agree	*N*	Disagree	*N*	Agree	*N*	Disagree
Do you think medical school faculty *should* be concerned about personal family situations of their students?	50	93%	4	7%	48	66%	25	34%	98	77%	29	23%*
I think that the medical faculty *actually* does show concern for my personal family situation.	30	56%	24	44%	20	27%	53	73%	50	39%	77	61%**

*$\chi^2 = 13.681$, 1 df, $p = 0.0011$
**$\chi^2 = 9.164$, 1 df, $p = 0.0025$

ville was reflected by the number and percentage of students who agreed that medical school faculty actually did show such concern. The difference was statistically significant between the two schools as determined from preclerkship (50 percent Louisville, 22 percent Pittsburgh) data ($p = 0.0027$).

Eight percent more students in Louisville agreed after the clerkship than before that faculty should be concerned (85 percent before clerkship, 93 percent after clerkship), whereas four percent fewer Pittsburgh students felt so after the clerkship than before (70 percent before, 66 percent after). Although 93 percent in Louisville agreed after the clerkship that medical school faculty should be concerned about personal family situations, only 56 percent perceived that the medical school faculty actually was concerned—a 37 percent difference. This is similar to the Pittsburgh students' responses to this item, of which 66 percent agreed that medical school faculty should be concerned and 27 percent agreed that the medical school faculty actually was concerned—a 36 percent difference.

DISCUSSION

The demographic profiles of the sample of 127 students reflect the current national average. In terms of the demographic and personal characteristics, there were no significant differences between the two schools. The differences in the curricula in the two schools should be noted when considering the results of the survey data.

In Pittsburgh, the students have an opportunity to learn intensely about a psychiatric subspecialty during their clerkship in addition to receiving somewhat more superficial exposure to a variety of subspecialties. The fact that The National Institute of Mental Health is also changing to specialty modules indicates that this concept is now nationally recognized as promoting scientific advances that have been lacking in psychiatry during previous decades. It is noteworthy that when individual items of the students' attitudes toward psychiatry are considered, the percentage of Pittsburgh students who think psychiatrists try to treat the whole patient and not just the disease decreases 17 percent when pre- and postclerkship data are compared. Along similar lines, 17 percent fewer Pittsburgh students agreed after their clerkship than before that psychiatric patients hardly ever get better. We could speculate that a higher percentage of students learned about improvement in patients whose specific disease entity was addressed on the specialty modules. Also, 7 percent fewer Pittsburgh students after the clerkship than before agreed that too little time was devoted to psychiatry.

The unique qualities of the Louisville curriculum seem to be reflected in the survey in different ways. In Louisville, there appears to be more emphasis on preventing stress in the students as well as in their significant others. Lectures are organized to offer the students information about the normal life cycle and human development, and experiences are offered to the students that contribute to understanding and care of patients as well as the students themselves and their significant others.

Major shifts were observed after the clerkship on the attitudinal survey. Twenty percent fewer agreed that psychiatric patients are not easy to like, 13 percent more agreed that psychiatrists are less dogmatic than are other doctors, 12 percent fewer agreed that psychiatrists tend to be more unstable than other doctors, and 22 percent more agreed that psychiatrists are in the forefront to humanize medicine. Seventeen percent more Louisville students agreed after the clerkship that too little time was spent on psychiatry.

Along these same dimensions, the percentage of students in Pittsburgh who agreed that psychiatric patients are not easy to like remained in the 20th percentile before and after the clerkship, those who agreed that psychiatrists are less dogmatic than other doctors remained in the 40th percentile before and after clerkship, and the group that agreed that psychiatrists tend to be more unstable than other doctors remained in the 20th percentile; those who agreed that psychiatrists are at the forefront of efforts to humanize medicine increased 14 percent.

Our survey confirms that the marketing efforts of the American Psychiatric Association (district and local chapters) on behalf of psychiatry are timely indeed. The percentage of students both in Louisville and Pittsburgh who agreed that psychiatrists are held in poor regard by most other doctors remained in the 60th percentile before and after the clerkship. Less than 10 percent considered psychiatrists failed physicians, although the percentage who agreed that this was the case increased five percent in each school when pre- and postclerkship surveys were compared. It would be of interest to determine in future data analysis how the replies of the five percent correlated with their other replies. It would also be of interest to interview those students to assess their concepts of physicians in general and themselves specifically as well as their particular lifetime experiences with psychiatrists.

It is also disconcerting to discover that 42 percent of the sample studied considered the families of schizophrenic patients "emotionally disturbed" and that the number of students with such a perception even increased slightly after the clerkship. Though most felt it was the physician's responsibility to address family issues of patients with schizophrenia, a high percentage (77 percent) felt they needed greater emphasis on various salient issues in order to feel more confident to develop a psychoeducational approach. Further analysis of the data will reveal which issues the students wanted to learn more about. Correlations of demographic data and various attitudes, and various attitudes with each other, have as yet not been performed. Further data analysis has the potential of impacting on the educational approach to medical students in psychiatry in a directed way.

The fact that all students agreed that psychiatric skills are essential in general practice is interesting. It should be noted that when the Sign test was applied to positive and negative attitudes toward psychiatry, the changes before and after the clerkship evened out, because fewer students had attitudes considered positive and fewer students had attitudes considered negative after the clerkship.

The statistically significant increase in percentage of Louisville students who agreed that empathy with patients is as important as factual knowledge in clinical medicine is indeed a tribute to the emphasis given such issues. The empathic and well-informed physician remains our ideal.

What have we learned in regard to our specific concern in this monograph, namely, whether medical students learn to be sensitive to and address concerns of families of schizophrenic patients? Our survey reveals that although none of the students agreed before the clerkship that family issues are the concern of the social worker only, four percent more in Louisville and eight percent more in Pittsburgh did after the clerkship. Whereas only six percent of the Louisville students and seven percent in Pittsburgh agreed before their clerkship that the physician's responsibility is toward the patient only, 15 percent in Louisville and 14 percent in Pittsburgh agreed with this after the clerkship. It is, of course, the word *only* that concerns us most in both situations. A multidisciplinary approach can be productive if each discipline can bring its own expertise to bear when dealing with patients and families so both can benefit from the new partnership with the mental health professional (which should include the patient's physician), who needs to know when psychiatric expertise for both patient and family are required.

This survey reveals three major issues that must be addressed on an ongoing basis:

1. Medical school faculty as a whole can contribute to improving the image of psychiatry.
2. Medical school curricula as a whole, and psychiatric clerkships in particular, need to identify methods whereby students are encouraged to treat patients and their families, to specialize in psychiatry to advance the field, and to acquire an interest to teach it to the other specialties.
3. Psychiatric faculty need to be in the forefront as role models for medical students in their approach to patients and families.

Our results indicate that we *can* train our nonpsychiatric student physicians to be empathic and competent in relating to families of the mentally ill. Our attitudes and use of non-jargon communication with the students and the patients we treat as the students observe us must be clear, useful, and exemplary. We must offer the students sufficient experiences in working with patients and with patients' families, with psychiatrists as role models who accomplish these two tasks well. The efforts of a multidisciplinary team need not diminish the role of the physician. We must emphasize the ways in which nonpsychiatric physicians can be effective with these families. All psychiatry clerks must be treated sensitively, and psychiatric concepts should be applied in other specialties. We must arrange for the students to learn about and participate in the family systems and the biopsychosocial approaches to therapy. We must provide useful psychoeducational material that these physicians can place in their office waiting rooms and libraries, such as *Living and Working With Schizophrenia* (23); *How You Can Help: A Guide for Families of Psychiatric Hospital Patients* (24); *Surviving Schizophrenia: A Family Manual* (25); *Family Care of Schizophrenia: A Problem-Solving Approach to the Treatment of Mental Illness* (26).

The students also must be taught how to find psychiatric referral sources when they enter practice or how to research questions when they enter academia. The physician's attitudes toward the schizophrenic patient and his or her family should be emphasized as an integral and vital part of the treatment and research process.

Just as students seek role models for wearing stethoscopes and starting IVs, they need role models to observe the biopsychosocial approach to physician–patient and physician–family interactions. The message to be constructive role models must go out to all staff, faculty, residents, secretaries, and cleaning staff. They must accept the responsiblity to be excellent role models for the students at all times.

We know from clinical research that constructively involving most families in the ongoing medical, including psychiatric, treatment of schizophrenic patients improves the patient's care and increases the chances for long-term remission. From this preliminary report, it appears that the medical students surveyed were ready and willing to learn the psychiatric skills necessary to be competent physicians in all specialties for this immensely needy patient and family population.

References

1. GMENAC: Summary Report of the Graduate Medical Education National Advisory Committee to the Secretary, Department of Health and Human Services. Washington DC, U.S. Department of Health and Human Services, Public Health Service Health Resources Administration, 1980

2. GPEP: Physicians for the Twenty-first Century: Report of the Panel on the General Professional Education of the Physician and College Preparation for Medicine. Washington DC, Association of American Medical Colleges, 1984

3. Hill D: Acceptance of psychiatry by the medical student. Br Med J 5177:917–918, 1960

4. Elizur A, Rosenheim E: Empathy and attitudes among medical students: the effects of group experience. J Med Educ 57:675–683, 1982

5. Maxmen JS: Student attitude changes during "psychiatric medicine" clerkships. Gen Hosp Psychiatry 1:98–103, 1979

6. Burra P, Kalin R, Leichner P, et al: The ATP 30—a scale for measuring medical students' attitudes to psychiatry. Med Educ 16:31–38, 1982

7. De-Nour A Kaplan, Weisstub EB: Attitudes of medical students toward people with emotional problems. Israeli Annals of Psychiatry and Related Disciplines 18:215–220, 1981

8. Antonovsky A: Training mental health care manpower: the medical student. Israeli Annals of Psychiatry and Related Disciplines 15:268–276, 1977

9. Maurice WL, Klonoff H, Miles JE, et al: Medical student change during a psychiatry clerkship: evaluation of a program. J Med Educ 50:181–189, 1975

10. Meltzer ML, Grigorian HM: Effect of psychiatric education on the attitudes of medical students to mental illness. Psychiatry 35:195–204, 1972

11. Arn L, Ottosson JO, Perris C: Attitudes toward mental disorders and mental care in university students. Int J Soc Psychiatry 17:270–276, 1971

12. Orleans CS, Houpt JL, Larson DB: Interpersonal factors in the psychiatry clerkship: new findings. Am J Psychiatry 137:1101–1103, 1980

13. Nielsen AC III, Eaton JS Jr.: Medical students' attitudes about psychiatry: implications for psychiatric recruitment. Arch Gen Psychiatry 38:1144–1154, 1981

14. Bashook PG, Weissman SH: Senior medical students' perceptions of the psychiatric clerkship. Am J Psychiatry 139:1614–1616, 1982

15. Yager J, LaMotte K, Nielsen A, et al: Medical students' evaluations of psychiatry: a cross-country comparison. Am J Psychiatry 139:1003–1009, 1982

16. Ghadirian AM, Engelsmann F: Medical students' attitudes toward psychiatry: a ten-year comparison. J Med Educ 16:39–43, 1982

17. Lau AY, Oxford DR: A study of student attitudes toward a psychiatric clerkship. J Med Educ 51:919–928, 1976

18. Johnson W, Snibbe J, Hoffman K, et al: Focused psychiatric curricular selection: student, psychiatrist, and non-psychiatrist expectations. Am J Psychiatry 134:1126–1130, 1977

19. Light D Jr: The impact of medical school on future psychiatrists. Am J Psychiatry 132:607–610, 1975

20. Yager J, LaMotte K, Fairbanks L: Medical student attitudes toward psychiatry in relation to psychiatric career choice. J Med Educ 57:949–951, 1982

21. Wilkinson DG, Greer S, Toone BK: Medical students' attitudes to psychiatry. Psychol Med 13:185–192, 1983

22. Wilkinson DG, Toone BK, Greer S: Medical students' attitudes to psychiatry at the end of the clinical curriculum. Psychol Med 13:655–658, 1983

23. Seeman M, Littman SK, Plummer E, et al: Living and Working With Schizophrenia. Toronto, University of Toronto Press, 1982

24. Korpell HS: How You Can Help: A Guide for Families of Psychiatric Hospital Patients. Washington DC, American Psychiatric Press, 1984

25. Torrey EF: Surviving Schizophrenia: A Family Manual. New York, Harper & Row, 1983

26. Falloon IRH, Boyd JL, McGill CW: Family Care of Schizophrenia: A Problem-Solving Approach to the Treatment of Mental Illness. New York, Guilford Press, 1984

Appendix

Name:____________________________ **Date:**________

Background Information

1. What were your undergraduate major and minor?
   Major ________________________ (subject)
   Minor ________________________ (subject)
2. As an undergraduate did you take any clinical psychology courses or basic psychology courses?
   _________ Number of courses
3. Are any of your family members or friends therapists or members of the psychiatric profession?
   ____Yes ____ No

	Friend	Relative	Nuclear Family Member
Psychiatrists			
Therapists			

4. Have you had a prior relationship(s) with a person who had a psychiatric disorder?
   ____Yes ____ No
5. If Yes, was this relationship with a
   ____ nuclear family member
   ____ relative
   ____ close friend
   ____ acquaintance
6. Did you ever work for pay or as a volunteer in a psychiatric hospital or a mental health unit?
   ____Yes ____ No
7. Do you intend to specialize in Psychiatry?
   ____ Yes, definitely ____ Doubtfully
   ____ Possibly ____ No, definitely

Attitudes Toward Psychiatry—
Pre- and Postclerkship

The following questionnaire is designed to measure the attitudes of students toward the field of psychiatry. On the following pages you will find eighteen (18) statements for which you will be asked to indicate your own agreement or disagreement. There are four possible answers/choices for each statement and you are asked to mark only one per statement. The answer categories are as follows:

A Strongly agree
B Mildly agree
C Mildly disagree
D Strongly disagree

Since this is an attitudinal questionnaire, it is important that your answers be extemporaneous (off-the-top-of-the-head) rather than deliberately thought out.

1. Psychiatric patients, generally speaking, are not easy to like. A B C D
2. Psychiatrists are, on the whole, less dogmatic than other doctors. A B C D
3. Psychiatrists tend to be more emotionally unstable than other doctors. A B C D
4. Psychiatrists are held in poor regard by most other doctors. A B C D
5. Psychiatrists try to treat the whole patient and not just the disease. A B C D
6. Psychiatrists are at the forefront of the movement to humanize medicine. A B C D
7. The problems presented by psychiatric patients are often particularly interesting and challenging. A B C D
8. Psychiatric patients hardly ever get better. A B C D

9. Psychiatric patients tend to make more emotional demands on their doctors than other patients. A B C D
10. Within medicine, psychiatry is one of the less important specialties. A B C D
11. Mental illness presents us with one of the great intellectual challenges in the field of medicine. A B C D
12. Psychiatry is too inexact; it seems to lack a proper scientific basis. A B C D
13. Psychiatrists are more concerned than other doctors to establish rapport with their patients. A B C D
14. Too little time is devoted to psychiatry in the medical curriculum. A B C D
15. Psychiatric skills are essential in general practice. A B C D
16. The practice of psychiatry is unrewarding because the treatment is so lengthy and the results so inconclusive. A B C D
17. Empathy with patients is as important as factual knowledge in clinical medicine. A B C D
18. Psychiatrists are often failed physicians. A B C D

Medical Student Questionnaire

Emphasis on maintaining patients with chronic schizophrenia in the community has prevailed for the past 20 years and will continue with the prevailing pressure to shorten expensive hospitalization. Mental health professionals other than the physician have been inclined to take over the caregiving role towards the families. Now that you have finished a rotation in psychiatry, we would like you to fill in the following questionnaire in an effort to assess:

1. what you have learned and would like to learn during your medical school education in regard to relating to families of patients with schizophrenia;
2. how you perceive your role as a practicing physician in regard to families of patients in general and to families of patients with schizophrenia in particular;
3. the role of personal, family, and social background in the approach of the physician to his/her patient.

______________________________ **Name**

Medical Student Questionnaire Preclerkship

We would like you to fill out the following questions. In order to enable us to compare your answers from before and after your clerkship, please put your *name* on each page.

Age:____
Gender: F__ M__
Marital status: S__ Engaged__ Div/Sep__ W__ Married__
Living with significant other__
How many children do you have? 0 1 2 3 4 5
I am considering ______________ or ______________
as my specialty.
I have not made up my mind yet. ____

Please check one:

1) The assessment of a patient with schizophrenia is very time-consuming and should be done only by a psychiatrist.
   Strongly Agree__ Agree__ Disagree__ Strongly Disagree__
2) The assessment and treatment of a patient with schizophrenia is emotionally draining.
   Strongly Agree__ Agree__ Disagree__ Strongly Disagree__
3) Families of schizophrenia patients are usually emotionally disturbed.
   Strongly Agree__ Agree__ Disagree__ Strongly Disagree__
4) In my opinion, the physician's responsibility is towards his/her patient only.
   Strongly Agree__ Agree__ Disagree__ Strongly Disagree__
5) In my opinion, it is the physician's responsibility to address family issues of patients with schizophrenia.
   Strongly Agree__ Agree__ Disagree__ Strongly Disagree__
6) In my opinion, family issues are the concern of the social worker only.
   Strongly Agree__ Agree__ Disagree__ Strongly Disagree__

7) Do you think that a medical school faculty *should* be concerned about the personal family situation of their students?
Strongly Agree__ Agree__ Disagree__ Strongly Disagree__

8) I think that the medical school faculty *actually* does show concern for my personal family situation.
Strongly Agree__ Agree__ Disagree__ Strongly Disagree__

9) Would you like to learn about:
a. Genetics of major mental illness
Yes__ Maybe__ No__ Don't know__
b. Community psychiatry issues
Yes__ Maybe__ No__ Don't know__
c. Family factors in relation to schizophrenia
Yes__ Maybe__ No__ Don't know__
d. Symptoms of schizophrenia and other mental disorders
Yes__ Maybe__ No__ Don't know__
e. Use of medication in schizophrenia and other mental disorders
Yes__ Maybe__ No__ Don't know__
f. Psychosocial interventions
Yes__ Maybe__ No__ Don't know__
g. Other
____
____
____
____

10) As a future physician, developing a psychoeducational approach to families of schizophrenic patients is a concern of mine.
Strongly Agree__ Agree__ Disagree__ Strongly Disagree__

11) I think a psychoeducational approach to families of schizophrenic patients can alleviate isolation and stress of family members.
Strongly Agree__ Agree__ Disagree__ Strongly Disagree__

12) I expect my rotation through psychiatry and lectures in psychiatry to make me more knowledgeable about and empathic with:

a. Schizophrenic patients

Strongly Agree__ Agree__ Disagree__ Strongly Disagree__

b. Families of schizophrenic patients

Strongly Agree__ Agree__ Disagree__ Strongly Disagree__

c. Both a and b

Strongly Agree__ Agree__ Disagree__ Strongly Disagree__

____________________________________ **Name**

Medical Student Questionnaire Postclerkship

We would like you to fill out the following questions. In order to enable us to compare your answers from before and after your clerkship, please put your *name* on each page.

My clinical home during the psychiatric rotation was ______
____
I plan to specialize in ________________________________
I am considering ____________________ or __________________
____ as my specialty.
I have not made up my mind yet _____

Check one:

1) The assessment of a patient with a schizophrenic or mental disorder is very time-consuming and should only be done by a psychiatrist.
   Strongly Agree__ Agree__ Disagree__ Strongly Disagree__
2) The assessment and treatment of a patient with schizophrenia is emotionally draining.
   Strongly Agree__ Agree__ Disagree__ Strongly Disagree__
3) Families of schizophrenic patients are usually emotionally disturbed.
   Strongly Agree__ Agree__ Disagree__ Strongly Disagree__
4) In my opinion, a physician's responsiblity is towards his/her patient only.
   Strongly Agree__ Agree__ Disagree__ Strongly Disagree__
5) In my opinion, it is the physician's responsiblity to address family issues of patients with schizophrenia.
   Strongly Agree__ Agree__ Disagree__ Strongly Disagree__
6) In my opinion, family issues are the concern of the social worker only.
   Strongly Agree__ Agree__ Disagree__ Strongly Disagree__

7) Do you think that a medical school faculty *should* be concerned about the personal family situation of their students?
Strongly Agree__ Agree__ Disagree__ Strongly Disagree__

8) I think that the medical school faculty *actually* does show concern for my personal family situation.
Strongly Agree__ Agree__ Disagree__ Strongly Disagree__

9) With regard to schizophrenia, do you think you would have liked to learn more about:
a. Genetics of major mental illness
Definitely__ Somewhat more__ Don't care__ Don't know__
b. Community psychiatry issues
Definitely__ Somewhat more__ Don't care__ Don't know__
c. Family factors in relation to schizophrenia
Definitely__ Somewhat more__ Don't care__ Don't know__
d. Symptoms of schizophrenia
Definitely__ Somewhat more__ Don't care__ Don't know__
e. Use of medication in schizophrenia
Definitely__ Somewhat more__ Don't care__ Don't know__
f. Psychosocial interventions
Definitely__ Somewhat more__ Don't care__ Don't know__
g. Other

10) More emphasis on one or more of the above would have made me more confident to develop a psychoeducational approach to families of schizophrenic patients.
Strongly Agree__ Agree__ Disagree__ Strongly Disagree__

11) I think a psychoeducational approach to families of schizophrenic patients can alleviate isolation and stress of family members.
Strongly Agree__ Agree__ Disagree__ Strongly Disagree__

12) My rotation through psychiatry and lectures in psychiatry have made me more knowledgeable and empathic about:
a. Schizophrenic patients
Strongly Agree__ Agree__ Disagree__ Strongly Disagree__
b. Families of schizophrenic patients
Strongly Agree__ Agree__ Disagree__ Strongly Disagree__
c. Both a and b
Strongly Agree__ Agree__ Disagree__ Strongly Disagree__